Insights You Need from
**Harvard
Business
Review**

CUSTOMER
DATA + PRIVACY

Insights You Need from Harvard Business Review

Business is changing. Will you adapt or be left behind?

Get up to speed and deepen your understanding of the topics that are shaping your company's future with the **Insights You Need from Harvard Business Review** series. Featuring HBR's smartest thinking on fast-moving issues—blockchain, cybersecurity, AI, and more—each book provides the foundational introduction and practical case studies your organization needs to compete today and collects the best research, interviews, and analysis to get it ready for tomorrow.

You can't afford to ignore how these issues will transform the landscape of business and society. The Insights You Need series will help you grasp these critical ideas—and prepare you and your company for the future.

Books in the series includes:

Agile

Artificial Intelligence

Blockchain

Climate Change

Coronavirus: Leadership and Recovery

Customer Data and Privacy

Cybersecurity

Monopolies and Tech Giants

Strategic Analytics

The Year in Tech 2021

Insights You Need from
Harvard Business Review

CUSTOMER DATA + PRIVACY

Harvard Business Review Press
Boston, Massachusetts

Copyright 2020 Harvard Business School Publishing Corporation
All rights reserved
Printed in the United States of America

10 9 8 7 6 5 4 3 2 1

No part of this publication may be reproduced, stored in or introduced into a retrieval system, or transmitted, in any form, or by any means (electronic, mechanical, photocopying, recording, or otherwise), without the prior permission of the publisher. Requests for permission should be directed to permissions@harvardbusiness.org, or mailed to Permissions, Harvard Business School Publishing, 60 Harvard Way, Boston, Massachusetts 02163.

The web addresses referenced in this book were live and correct at the time of the book's publication but may be subject to change.

Library of Congress Cataloging-in-Publication Data

Names: Harvard Business Review Press.
Title: Customer data and privacy : the insights you need from Harvard Business Review.
Other titles: Insights you need from Harvard Business Review.
Description: Boston, Massachusetts : Harvard Business Review Press, [2020] | Series: Insights you need from Harvard Business Review | Includes index.
Identifiers: LCCN 2020013620 (print) | LCCN 2020013621 (ebook) | ISBN 9781633699861 (paperback) | ISBN 9781633699878 (ebook)
Subjects: LCSH: Data protection. | Privacy, Right of.
Classification: LCC QA76.9.A25 C875 2020 (print) | LCC QA76.9.A25 (ebook) | DDC 005.8—dc23
LC record available at https://lccn.loc.gov/2020013620
LC ebook record available at https://lccn.loc.gov/2020013621

The paper used in this publication meets the requirements of the American National Standard for Permanence of Paper for Publications and Documents in Libraries and Archives Z39.48-1992

Contents

Contents

Introduction

TRUST

The New Competitive Advantage

by Timothy Morey

Imagine you're a parent taking your teenage daughter to a beach volleyball training session. As you're getting ready to leave the house, you ask Alexa about the weather. You punch the address into Google Maps to check traffic conditions; your Tesla Model 3 knows where you're going and who's driving. En route, license plate scanners assess tolls and track your progress. On arrival, you pay for street parking with the ParkMobile app and use the Starbucks app to pick up coffee. You're not even two hours into a Saturday morning and already Amazon, Google, Tesla, the local government, AT&T, a parking app provider, Starbucks,

Apple, and a payment provider know where you are and what you're up to. And that's before any of them sell your information to data brokers.

Until recently, consumers have been largely unaware, indifferent, or resigned to the use of their data for personalized experiences and targeted marketing. The convenience outweighed the cost, resulting in the *privacy paradox*, where consumers *say* they are concerned but don't change their behavior. But the sheer pervasiveness of digital surveillance is causing concerned customers to act and call into question how companies treat their data.

Governments have stepped up regulation in response to data breaches and abuses, from the General Data Protection Regulation (GDPR) in Europe to the California Consumer Privacy Act (CCPA) in the United States. Regulatory backlash is just one of the costs of abusing customer data. It also results in reputational damage, direct costs to businesses to deal with the cleanup of data breaches, and executive job losses all the way up to the CEO. Data breaches and abuses make it harder for businesses to attract and retain talented employees. But most of all, mistreating customer data results in wary customers and a loss of trust. If customers don't trust you, they're less likely to do business with you. More than ever, consumer trust matters.

Companies that are trusted can gather more personal data and use that data to enhance their services, giving them a competitive advantage over less trusted firms. And trusted companies are more readily forgiven when things inevitably go wrong. Take the smart speaker market: Amazon's Alexa dominates with 70% share, whereas Facebook's Portal, despite a quality product and a massive marketing push, remains statistically insignificant. That's no surprise, considering the number and magnitude of data breaches Facebook has suffered. Unfortunately, trust does not easily lend itself to business metrics and KPIs. Rather, it must be measured indirectly through customer attrition, share of customer wallet, customer lifetime value, and attitudinal metrics such as Net Promoter Scores. Trust resides in customers' minds, formed by their perceptions and experiences of a company over time. It's not entirely in a company's control; however, companies *can* take steps to increase their chances of being trusted.

So beyond meeting basic regulatory requirements, how can your company build trust with its customers?

Be clear about your data practices

Don't obfuscate your data practices with legalese; honestly explain your policy in clear and simple language. A short video, perhaps from your CEO, is better than asking customers to click away an "I accept" privacy notice that never gets read. On top of building trust, companies with clear statements are less likely to be punished by consumers if and when they suffer a data breach.

Give your customers control

Providing your customers with tools to manage how they interact with your company and being upfront about what you do with their data builds trust. It signals to customers that you're respectful of their wishes and will be thoughtful stewards of their data. Offer an easy-to-navigate privacy dashboard, promote and link to it, and allow customers to download or erase their data.

Make it a two-way street

Even though the direct-exchange mechanism between consumers and providers has broken down to some extent, trusted companies offer clear value to their customers in exchange for their data. Businesses like Spotify and Pinterest curate recommendations as they observe user behavior, giving consumers clear benefits for taking the time to listen to or like content. The more value a company provides, and the more consistently it provides it, the more it will be trusted. Trust has evolved from a rational evaluation of a business's trustworthiness to a more emotional evaluation, rather like brand perception.

Go beyond the legally required minimum

Data-driven technology firms abused consumer trust through their cavalier attitudes to privacy in the first years of the 2000s and into the early 2010s. That's now catching up with them as a subset of privacy-active consumers switch providers over data policies. It's also driving new regulation beyond the GDPR and CCPA. As other types of businesses and industries digitize their customer experience, they're dealing with skeptical consumers who've been abused by data-driven tech firms. To navigate this effectively and to build trust, collect only the data your company needs, educate customers about how you're going to use the data, and behave in a customer-centric fashion.

Where do we go from here?

Regulation will remain in place and, if anything, become stricter. The hands-off approach to regulation of early internet businesses has given way to a realization that consumer protections are needed. For businesses coping with regulation, the typical approach is to meet the demands of the strictest jurisdiction and make that the global standard for the company. There's little interest in maintaining one digital product for California, another for the rest of the United States, yet another for the European Union, and so on.

Business appetite for customer data will continue to grow. Access to data will increase competitive advantage as businesses with data can offer valuable, tailored, personal experiences to their customers. In retrospect, offering targeted advertising was easy, because it used data that wasn't particularly sensitive. What comes next will be harder. Health care applications that are based on medical records and DNA, wellness products that ask for a customer's mental health history, or financial products that rely on full disclosures of spending histories will all require access to much more sensitive data sets. Companies that have proved themselves to be trustworthy will do better here.

The big unknown is how peoples' attitudes toward data privacy will evolve. But for business decision making, it's safest to assume that customer skepticism will grow. Businesses need to take action today to remain on the right side of emerging customer expectations. The chapters in this volume will help you think critically about the steps your organization needs to take to collect, store, and use customer data in a way that builds trust—and your business.

Further Reading

If after reading this book, you want to dig deeper, I recommend the following resources:

The Age of Surveillance Capitalism: The Fight for a Human Future at the New Frontier of Power, by Shoshana Zuboff (PublicAffairs, 2020).

What Stays in Vegas: The World of Personal Data— Lifeblood of Big Business—and the End of Privacy as We Know It, by Adam Tanner (PublicAffairs, 2016).

Electronic Frontier Foundation (EFF) (https://www.eff.org/) advocates for internet civil liberties. It publishes articles and white papers on privacy, free speech, and innovation, advocating for ordinary technology users. As you make product and service design decisions, it's useful to ask yourself what EFF would say about your choices.

Insights You Need from
Harvard Business Review

CUSTOMER DATA + PRIVACY

UNINFORMED CONSENT

by Leslie K. John

The satirical website the *Onion* once ran an article with the headline "Woman Stalked Across 8 Websites by Obsessed Shoe Advertisement." Everywhere she went online, this fictional consumer saw the same ad. "The creepiest part," she says in the story, "is that it even seems to know my shoe size." The piece poked fun at an increasingly common—if clumsy—digital marketing technique. But today its gentle humor seems almost quaint. Technology has advanced far beyond the browser cookies and retargeting that allow ads to follow us around the internet. Smartphones now track our physical location and proximity to other people—and, as researchers recently discovered, can even do so when we turn off location services.[1] We can disable the tracking on our web browsers, but our digital fingerprints can still be connected across devices, enabling our identities to be sleuthed out. Home assistants like Alexa listen to our conversations and, when activated, record what we're saying. A growing range of everyday *things*—from Barbie dolls to medical devices—connect to the internet and transmit information about our movements, our behavior, our preferences, and even our health. A dominant web business model today is to amass as much data on individuals as possible and then use it or sell it—to target or persuade, reward or penalize. The internet has become a surveillance economy.

What's more, the rise of data science has made the information collected much more powerful, allowing companies to build remarkably detailed profiles of individuals. Machine learning and artificial intelligence can make eerily accurate predictions about people using seemingly random data. Companies can use data analysis to deduce someone's political affiliation or sexuality or even who has had a one-night stand. As new technologies such as facial recognition software and home DNA testing are added to the tool kit, the surveillance done by businesses may soon surpass that of the 20th century's most invasive security states.

The obvious question is, How could consumers let this happen? As a behavioral scientist, I study how people sometimes act against their own interests. One issue is that "informed consent"—the principle companies use as permission to operate in this economy—is something of a charade. Most consumers are either unaware of the personal information they share online or, quite understandably, unable to determine the cost of sharing it—if not both.

It's true that consumers do gain some benefits from all the data gathering, such as more meaningful advertising and better customer service, pricing, and potentially even access to credit. But companies urgently need to find a way to balance the benefits with privacy protection. Consumer advocates are raising alarm bells about invasive digital practices. Public outcries ensue each time a scandal hits the headlines, whether it involves Equifax's loss of sensitive personal information about tens of millions of people or Russian operatives using social media to manipulate the votes of Americans. Internet privacy experts who not too long ago were viewed as cranks on the fringe now testify before Congress and headline conferences. In Europe major legislation to protect user privacy has already passed. We're starting to see signs of a widespread "techlash," which could have profound implications for firms that use consumers' data. It's probably no coincidence that Facebook saw its valuation plummet roughly 20% after it publicly suggested it might scale back on some data collection.

At the same time, consumers don't reward companies for offering better privacy protection. Privacy-enhancing technologies have not been widely adopted. People are generally unwilling to pay for privacy-enhancing technologies and, even if they do, will pay only modest amounts.[2] Though some might take this as evidence that people simply don't care about privacy, I've come to a different conclusion: People *do* care, but as I'll explain, several factors impede their ability to make wise choices.

If both sides continue on these diverging trajectories, the surveillance economy may be headed for a market failure. The good news is that policy makers can help. The first step is to understand how people make decisions about the privacy of their personal information and how they can be induced to overshare.

How Consumers Got In So Deep

Let's be frank: People are bad at making decisions about their private data. They misunderstand both costs and benefits. Moreover, natural human biases interfere with their judgment. And whether by design or accident, major platform companies and data aggregators have structured their products and services to exploit those biases, often in subtle ways.

Impatience

People tend to overvalue immediate costs and benefits and underweight those that will occur in the future. They want $9 today rather than $10 tomorrow. On the internet, this tendency manifests itself in a willingness to reveal personal information for trivial rewards. Free quizzes and surveys are prime examples. Often administered by third parties, they are a data-security nightmare, but many people can't resist them. For instance, on the popular "real age" website, people divulge a large amount of sensitive health information in exchange for the immediate "benefit" of knowing whether their "biological age" is older or younger than their calendar age. Consumers gain zero financial reward for such disclosures. They may be vaguely aware of the potential costs of providing such information (at its extreme, higher insurance premiums down the road), but because those downsides are vague and in the future, they're disregarded in exchange for a few minutes of fun.

Impatience also prevents us from adopting privacy controls. In one experiment, people who were setting up a digital wallet were offered a service that would secure (that is, encrypt) their purchase transaction data.[3] Adding the service took a few additional steps, but only a quarter of people successfully went through them. The vast majority were unwilling to trivially inconvenience themselves by following a onetime simple process in order to protect their data from abuse down the road.

Data "transactions" are often structured so that the benefits of disclosure are immediate, tangible, and attractive, while the costs are delayed and more amorphous— and in these situations, our impatience tilts us toward disclosure. Mobile credit-card stations, for instance, email you receipts and make transactions fast and paperless. But the costs of companies' capturing your email address and other personal information come later. Sensitive data, such as your name, demographics, and location, is amassed and shared or sold, and in all likelihood you are eventually barraged with targeted marketing. Although some of those ads may be welcome, others may be annoying or intrusive. And some fear that in the future consumer data may even be used in more-impactful ways, such as credit score calculations—and possibly lead to discriminatory "digital redlining."[4]

The endowment effect

In theory people should be willing to pay the same amount to buy a good as they'd demand when selling it. In reality, people typically value a good *less* when they have to buy it. A similar dynamic can be seen when people make decisions about privacy.

In one study, Alessandro Acquisti, George Loewenstein, and I offered consumers one of two gift cards: a $10 "private" card that wouldn't track their purchases or a $12 card that would.[5] In some cases the study's subjects were given the option to "buy" privacy by trading the $12 tracked card for the $10 untracked card. In other cases they were given the option to "sell" their privacy by trading the $10 card for the $12 one. In either situation, privacy cost $2. Surely your willingness to forgo $2 to protect your privacy should not be affected by which card you're initially handed. But, in fact, almost 50% of people were willing to give up privacy for $2, but fewer than 10% were willing to pay $2 to get privacy.

This implies that we value privacy less when we have to acquire it. So something as simple as whether our information is by default public or private can have enormous implications; we're far more amenable to sharing it when the default is public. More broadly, the disparity

7

is consistent with the way privacy breaches generate outcry, while privacy gains aren't met with commensurate jubilation. It may also set the stage for vicious cycles of privacy erosion: Breaches make information increasingly public. And when our information is public, we value our privacy less, in turn making us more comfortable with parting with it.

Firms have made loose privacy defaults, well, the default for the tech industry. Here are just a few examples: In November 2016, Uber changed its preset options to allow it to track users at all times. (It changed them back in September 2017 after facing criticism.) On the social payments app Venmo, transactions are public by default. Google automatically stores your location when you merely open its Maps app; opting out is confusing, if not downright misleading.

Users' ability to opt out is also often obfuscated. In a recent white paper, Senator Mark Warner (D-VA) highlighted how Facebook's mobile app used defaults to "deceptively prod users into consenting to upload their phone contacts to Facebook (something highly lucrative to Facebook in tracking a user's 'social graph')."[6] The first screen on the mobile app gives the impression that consent to sharing contacts is the sole choice. Only when users click on a "learn more" button do they discover (if they scroll down and look carefully) that they can opt out.

Illusion of control

People share a misapprehension that they can control chance processes. This explains why, for example, study subjects valued lottery tickets that they had personally selected more than tickets that had been randomly handed to them.[7] People also confuse the superficial trappings of control with real control. In a study on receptiveness to behaviorally targeted ads, Tami Kim, Kate Barasz, and I found that people are more comfortable with third-party data sharing, a practice they ordinarily deem invasive, when they have a sense of control—even if what they seem to control has nothing to do with the ads they see or the data shared. People can be put at ease by something as irrelevant as a reminder that they can choose their profile pictures. Related research suggests that people are overconfident about their ability to control their own security in cyberspace. In a recent survey conducted by Experian, 56% of respondents mistakenly believed that the risk of identity theft decreases over time, and 10% believed that they weren't at risk because their finances were weak.

While some efforts to grant consumers more control over their data are meaningful, I also see instances in which their privacy concerns may be placated by an illusory sense of control. Consider the Network Advertising

Initiative's Consumer Opt Out site. On it people are informed of the companies that are customizing ads for their browsers and can select which companies' to opt out of. When I used the service, I opted out of 72 firms' ads. I felt in control. But when I checked the fine print, I learned that my choice only prevents the specific companies from delivering targeted advertisements; it doesn't necessarily stop me from being tracked—a fact that's easily forgotten because I no longer see those targeted ads—the very thing that could remind me my data is being collected.

Desire for disclosure

This is not a decision-making bias. Rather, humans have what appears to be an innate desire, or even need, to share with others. After all, that's how we forge relationships—and we're inherently social creatures. In one study, even people who were very concerned about their privacy went on to readily divulge personal information to a chat bot. Unloading your secrets has psychological and physical benefits.[8] When strangers are paired up in lab experiments and prompted to disclose personal information with each other, they build greater rapport.[9] Keeping a journal in which you share your worries can improve physical health, while keeping secrets can reduce well-being.[10] And a neuroscientific study found that when people disclose information about themselves, it activates the reward regions in their brains; in the same experiment, people even passed up monetary rewards for the chance to answer personal questions.[11]

Our orientation toward disclosure is also apparent in how we perceive those who abstain: We view people who withhold with contempt. For example, as my research with Kate Barasz and Mike Norton shows, we dislike and distrust those who avoid answering personal questions *even more* than those who reveal damaging information about themselves. In one experiment, participants indicated greater interest in hiring a job candidate who admitted to having done drugs than someone who had withheld the answer to a question about drug use.

Online, the boundaries between social and commercial transactions are increasingly blurred. For example, on virtually all social media platforms, ads resemble noncommercial posts. Though there may be other reasons for this practice (the wish to make ads less intrusive, for instance), it also gives ads the feel of social posts, which I suspect helps trigger people's desire to disclose and keeps privacy concerns at bay. Similarly, casual, unprofessional-looking interfaces induce self-disclosure too, even though such interfaces are often indicative of poorer privacy protections.[12]

Indeed, heightening the desire to disclose appears to be central to many social media sites, right down to the perpetual "What's on your mind?" prompt on Facebook. Online retailers have been adding similar social elements to sales processes, such as robot chat agents designed to build rapport with consumers. The structure of Venmo's site mirrors that of social media sites. Users build their social graph by adding contacts; those contacts' transactions are displayed prominently in a newsfeed. That makes financial transactions feel like social transactions, turning something that people would ordinarily keep private into something that they not only are comfortable sharing but potentially *want* to share. Though consumers may get some value out of sites' social aspects, those aspects can also make the risks of disclosure less apparent.

False sense of boundaries

In offline contexts, people naturally understand and comply with social norms about discretion and interpersonal communication. Though we may be tempted to gossip about someone, the norm "don't talk behind people's backs" usually checks that urge. Most of us would never tell a trusted confidant our secrets when others are within earshot. And people's reactions in the moment can make us quickly scale back if we disclose something inappropriate.

But in the online world, the rules are different. We often don't get the same rich, visceral feedback that tempers our behavior in the offline world. We may have the illusion, for instance, that we're disclosing information only to a select group of people, such as the friends in our social media feed. People get into trouble when they post rants (say, about their employer) meant for a small subset of their friends, forgetting the broader audience that can see those disclosures (say, their boss and colleagues).

We're easily seduced by the seeming ephemerality of digital interactions, too. My research with Reto Hofstetter and Roland Rüppell has found that temporary sharing technologies that allow messages to disappear, such as Snapchat and Instagram Stories, lead people to make uninhibited disclosures. Yet the damage to their reputations is potentially long lasting. Most of us wouldn't dream of making a profane gesture in a professional meeting just because such an act would be fleeting. But online, perhaps because we often receive only impoverished feedback, the promise of ephemerality goads us into oversharing.

Complexity and the Coming Conundrum

We've unpacked both the consumer and producer sides of the surveillance economy, but underlying it all is a factor of increasing importance: complexity.

Do you know how cookies work? Do you understand how information on your browsing history, search requests, Facebook likes, and so on are monetized and exchanged among brokers to target advertising to you? Do you know what's recorded and tracked when you ask your digital assistant to do something? The answer is probably no. That's a problem.

A key tenet of any functioning market is "buyer beware." But online, weighing the risks against the benefits of sharing can feel like an act of futile metaphysics. How much privacy have you lost when firms track your location—and what is the value of that privacy? Is it worth the added convenience of a GPS navigation tool? What should a consumer be "paid" for allowing continuous location tracking? Moreover, the behind-the-scenes "plumbing" of the surveillance economy is so byzantine and opaque that it's effectively impossible for consumers to be adequately informed.

There is also no way to know what all third parties are doing, or will do, with your data. Although Facebook has been tightening oversight of apps as well as their access to user data, the fact is that many apps have been selling user information obtained on Facebook, and consumers can't possibly have known where their data would end up when they agreed to the apps' terms and conditions. Suppose that a couple of years ago you clicked on a Facebook link for a quiz like "What '80s Movie Best Represents Your Life?" The administrator of the quiz could have gathered some Facebook data—birthday, friends, things you've clicked on, likes, locations, groups you belonged to, where you'd checked in—and made it available to third parties by wrapping it in JavaScript, circumventing privacy protections offered by most web browsers. A data broker could have collected that parcel of information and sold it for use in targeted ad campaigns. It would be effectively impossible for you to figure out how your data moved through the advertising ecosystem or identify the brokers or agencies involved.

There's also nothing stopping your friends from sharing information on your behalf. In a study by economists Susan Athey, Christian Catalini, and Catherine Tucker, people readily disclosed their friends' email addresses in exchange for free pizza.

Even when consumers actively seek to uncover what personal information about them has been shared and with which entities, firms are not always forthcoming. When users click on Facebook's "Why am I seeing this ad?" feature (which is difficult to find), the explanations they're given are sometimes uselessly generic (for example, "One reason you're seeing this ad is that Rothy's wants to reach people who may be similar to their customers").

Even if all the players and transactions in the surveillance economy were widely understood, consumers would still sometimes find it impossible to know what they were actually disclosing, because discrete pieces of data can be synthesized to form new data. For example, it is possible to identify someone by knowing the dates and locations of just four of his credit card transactions. A person's Social Security number can sometimes be predicted by her birth date and birthplace, meaning that if a consumer provides her birth date to an entity that already knows her birthplace, she may unwittingly divulge her Social Security number. What the consumer reveals is not just a function of what the consumer *decides* to reveal. It's also determined by what the receiver knows about that consumer.

Algorithms and processing power now make it possible to build behavioral profiles of users without ever having to ask for their data. Their mere presence in someone's social network or comment on someone else's social feed can be harvested to predict and profile. This phenomenon creates entirely new conundrums: If a company profiles a consumer using machine learning, is that profile subject to the regulatory rules of personally identifiable information? Does the consumer have any right to it? Should a company be allowed to use such techniques without the consent of the targets, or at all? No one knows.

For all these reasons, privacy decision making is incredibly complex. And when people perceive decisions to be overwhelmingly complex, they are prone to disengage. Anyone faced with the decision to "accept" online terms of use can relate. They are typically so long that you cannot reasonably expect anyone to read them, let alone understand them. One study estimated it would take Americans 54 billion hours annually to read the privacy policy of every new website they visit.[13]

So most consumers respond by throwing their hands up and agreeing to terms that would give them pause if they understood them. Mobile game app users, for example, might be surprised to learn that they have "consented" to allow some of these apps to share their personal data with third parties, for any reason whatever. Some even have access to people's microphones, which they use to record audio *even when the app is not in use—and even though that information is not used in the game itself.* "Super apps" like China's WeChat, which has one billion users, have far-reaching access to personal data, including social media posts, bank and credit card details, financial transactions, and even voice data. By technically providing information on the costs and benefits of information sharing and having consumers "agree" to it, these and other digital platforms maintain a kind of plausible deniability.

Complexity makes it hard to fix the surveillance economy without breaking the system entirely. Though that's a possible outcome, it's not a good one. Data gathering doesn't have to be a bad deal for internet users. Consumers have gained enormous benefits from it and from major platform companies such as Alphabet and Facebook. However, the fact that so much of the surveillance economy operates surreptitiously and by default suggests that tech companies have reason to fear consumers might not opt in if they truly understood the bargain that "free" technologies entailed.

Moreover, while consumers surf in the dark, firms have a much better understanding of their own costs and benefits. Expenses for tracking technology and data brokers and the lift in sales from more finely targeted ads can be calculated with precision. Firms thus have an informational advantage over consumers. As any economist will tell you, that asymmetry on its own suggests a market failure and thus invites regulatory intervention.

Restoring Balance

In the 1960s the United States and other governments began to systematically write product safety regulations after it became clear that consumers couldn't properly assess risks—such as the danger of riding in a car without a seat belt and the chance that a soda bottle might explode—and that firms weren't motivated to address them. Scholars have argued that in such situations it makes sense for regulators to shift risk onto those best able to manage it: the makers of the products. Given that consumers face similar challenges in evaluating privacy risks, lawmakers should consider taking this approach with regulations about personal data collection.

Of course, any regulatory response will prompt skeptics to point out the thorny issues we haven't yet begun to understand well. Here are just a few of the questions they're apt to raise:

- To what extent do people own their personal data?

- Should people have an expectation of privacy in public spaces, or is anything they do in public fair game for surveillance?

- Is the online realm a public space?

- What is the value of privacy? Can it even be calculated?

- What is the value of personal information? Can it even be calculated?

- What information is mine to control—does it include AI-generated predictions about my behavior?

- What are the costs of enforcing privacy regulation? Do they outweigh the benefits?

Some argue that it may be too late to protect consumers' personal data, because it has already been fed into machine-learning tools that can accurately infer information about us without collecting any more. Despite machine learning's impressive capabilities, this is not yet the reality. Firms continue to have great interest in obtaining consumer data. But even if predictive AI capabilities do dampen the demand for consumer data, regulation could place basic limits on what firms could do with those predictions (by, say, preventing health insurers from using them to discriminate against applicants who might have medical problems). (See the sidebar "Why Is Data Governance So Hard?")

Though the details of such regulation are beyond the scope of this chapter, the research I've described does provide some broad guidance about what is likely to work. First, the goal should not be simply to make it harder to share or to unilaterally increase firms' barriers to consumer data. Such an approach would be overly simplistic, because firms and consumers alike have much to gain from sharing information. Regulators should also be aware of the costs of restricting information flow—for example, the potential to impede innovation.

Why Is Data Governance So Hard?

by Bhaskar Chakravorti

As we consider the future of data governance, we're missing a system that defines and grants users "digital agency"— the ability to own the rights to their personal data, manage access to this data, and potentially be compensated fairly for such access. This would make data similar to other forms of personal property: a home, a bank account, or even a mobile phone number.

But data, unlike other forms of personal property, is just plain complicated. Any workable solution would need to manage the following 10-point checklist at a minimum:

1. Define what constitutes the personal data to which a user has exclusive rights. For example, a personal photo may contain a picture of a friend tagged by the user. Moving that data could violate the friend's privacy. Alternatively, a user's click trail tracked by a platform reveals the user's preferences based on the platform's analysis. At what point does that revelation become the platform's intellectual property?

(Continued)

Why Is Data Governance So Hard?

2. Establish criteria to demarcate personal data, anonymized data, and third-party data. To see why this can be difficult, even anonymized data when linked can reveal personally identifiable information; an algorithm was shown to identify 99.98% of Americans by knowing as few as 15 demographic attributes per person. Alternatively, if a user's data links to third-party data that is deemed harmful or false, can the user remove it without violating the third party's free-speech rights?

3. Create a transparent, market-based, and universally accepted system of valuing data and compensating users accordingly for trading data. The compensation could be in the form of a tailored service or monetary compensation, while some data may not be tradable at all.

4. Define standards for how the data is stored, moved, or accessed interoperably across different digital platforms.

5. Establish criteria to evaluate the trade-offs between many needs: interoperability, privacy, and cybersecurity. Ease of interoperability, for example, could also reduce cybersecurity.

6. Establish criteria to evaluate the trade-offs between personal data and the use of aggregated data as a public good—for training algorithms for societal use, fraud detection, public safety, flagging fake news, and so on.

7. Mitigate the transaction costs of negotiating with multiple parties whenever a platform needs multiple data sources—for example, location data needed for a ride-sharing app.

8. Mitigate the risks of bots or malicious actors taking advantage of compensation for access to data. For example, Microsoft experimented with paying users for data, and bots—with no usable information—exploited the system.

9. Make it easy to move data across platforms, without expecting the user to be a technology expert.

10. Anticipate unintended consequences of changes as fundamental as transferring the control and management of data from big tech professionals to regular users.

(Continued)

Why Is Data Governance So Hard?

Finding a workable digital agency solution is daunting. It's time to figure out which parts of this checklist are most practical, scalable, and sustainable.

Bhaskar Chakravorti is the dean of Global Business at the Fletcher School at Tufts University and founding executive director of Fletcher's Institute for Business in the Global Context. He is the author of *The Slow Pace of Fast Change*.

Source: Adapted from "Why It's So Hard for Users to Control Their Data" by Bhaskar Chakravorti, published on hbr.org on January 30, 2020 (reprint #H05DVB)

In Europe, the General Data Protection Regulation (GDPR) privacy law requires firms to get consumers' opt-in consent to harvest personal information. This is laudable because it addresses issues with defaults, though at the cost of annoying and inconveniencing consumers. And when people are repeatedly faced with decisions about opting in or out, they can become desensitized, which is hardly a recipe for thoughtful choices. So some of the same factors that make data collection ripe for intervention also make designing regulations about it particularly challenging.

A common approach is to require firms to give consumers information on the relevant costs and benefits of sharing and to tell them about data breaches. But as I've noted, research points to the limits of this approach. It's unlikely to solve the problem given that users don't read privacy policies and, despite the media uproar, don't take much action when they learn of breaches. (Indeed, the majority of Facebook users stayed on the platform after the Cambridge Analytica scandal broke.)

A related approach is to use regulation to directly reduce risks to consumers by, say, placing specific restrictions on what personal data firms can collect and how they can use it, and handing out penalties for noncompliance. In the United States, there is no national law regulating the collection and use of personal data. Some basic ground rules do seem to be in order. In Massachusetts, for example, companies must encrypt personal data that flows over public networks. And California's groundbreaking Consumer Privacy Act imposes several rules on firms; for example, businesses that sell consumers' data must allow users to opt out of such sales without penalty.

But a problem with this approach is that it can lead to the "Whack-A-Mole" problem, whereby firms find loopholes to wriggle out of while complying with the letter of the law. For example, California's privacy law forbids differential treatment of consumers who exercise their privacy rights—unless it "is reasonably related to the value provided by the consumer's data"—a possible loophole for firms to exploit. And workarounds may be particularly easy to find in the digital space, where firms are quite nimble; a quick tweak in wording of a privacy policy can have enormous consequences.

So the real promise of government intervention may lie in giving firms an incentive to use consumers' personal data only in reasonable ways. One way to do that is to adopt a tool used in the product safety regime: strict liability, or making firms responsible for negative consequences arising from their use of consumer data, even in the absence of negligence or ill intent. Relatedly, firms that collect our personal data could be deemed, as legal scholars Jack Balkin and Jonathan Zittrain have argued, "information fiduciaries"—entities that have a legal obligation to behave in a trustworthy manner with our data. Interventions such as these would give firms a sincere interest in responsibly using data and in preempting abuses and failures in the system of data collection and sharing (because otherwise they'd face financial penalties).

To be sure, many difficult questions need to be answered first. For example, how would damages be determined? Although the harm done by disclosure cannot be calculated with precision, it could be estimated. Terry Bollea (also known as "Hulk Hogan") was awarded $115 million in compensatory damages when Gawker violated his privacy by posting a sex tape of him where millions could see it. (Full disclosure: I worked as a consultant to Bollea's team on this case.)

Another challenge is proving harm; because this is hard to do in the privacy sphere, some have cogently argued, the courts would have to accept the notion of probabilistic damages. Also, what constitutes reasonable versus unreasonable data use? That's difficult to articulate, but it's often the kind of thing you know when you see it. And a key aim of regulation would be to serve as a deterrent and prevent irresponsible use of data in the first place.

A common concern with regulation is that it can reduce competition. The cost of compliance is disproportionately burdensome for small players, so the net effect of regulation can be greater market power for large incumbents. But there is reason to believe that this pitfall would be less likely if firms were given an interest in behaving in a trustworthy manner. First, companies with deep pockets would be disproportionately targeted by those seeking damages. Second, this approach is conceivably less restrictive to new entrants because it need not require the large up-front investment in compliance that direct approaches typically do.

Regulation is not a panacea for the surveillance economy. It will surely introduce some new issues. There's also more to gaining consumers' trust than merely following the law. But if we draw on insights from behavioral science and accept that consumers are imperfect decision makers rather than perfectly rational economic actors, we can design better regulation that will help realize the benefits of data collection while mitigating its pitfalls—for both firms and consumers alike.

Data gathering doesn't have to be exploitative or creepy for internet users, but companies need to find ways to balance the benefits of collection with privacy protection for consumers. Companies and policy makers should consider these guidelines when developing regulations:

- ✓ Shape solutions after product safety regulations (such as "Caution: This coffee may be hot") since most consumers aren't skilled at evaluating privacy risks.

- ✓ Flip the model and ask customers to *opt in* and consent to the harvesting of their personal information.

- ✓ Require firms to give consumers information on the relevant costs and benefits of sharing and to tell them about data breaches. And government intervention should help make this a two-way street by giving firms an incentive to use consumers' personal data only in fair ways.

✓ Place restrictions on data-harvesting practices that are risky for consumers, and penalize noncomplying companies.

NOTES

1. Olivia Krauth, "Your Smartphone Can Be Tracked Even If GPS, Location Services Are Turned Off," *TechRepublic*, February 8, 2018, https://www.techrepublic.com/article/your-smartphone-can -be-tracked-even-if-gps-location-services-are-turned-off/.

2. Janice Y. Tsai, Serge Egelman, Lorrie Cranor, and Alessandro Acquisti, "The Effect of Online Privacy Information on Purchasing Behavior: An Experimental Study," *Information Systems Research* 22, no. 2 (2011): 254–268.

3. Susan Athey, Christian Catalini, and Catherine E. Tucker, "The Digital Privacy Paradox: Small Money, Small Costs, Small Talk," MIT Sloan Research Paper No. 5196-17, Stanford University Graduate School of Business Research Paper No. 17-14, February 15, 2017; revised April 17, 2018, https://papers.ssrn.com/sol3/papers .cfm?abstract_id=2916489.

4. Robinson Meyer, "Could a Bank Deny Your Loan Based on Your Facebook Friends?," *Atlantic*, September 25, 2015, https:// www.theatlantic.com/technology/archive/2015/09/facebooks-new -patent-and-digital-redlining/407287/.

5. Alessandro Acquisti, Leslie K. John, and George Loewenstein, "What Is Privacy Worth?," *Journal of Legal Studies* 42, no. 2 (June 2013): 249–274.

6. Mark R. Warner, "Potential Policy Proposals for Regulation of Social Media and Technology Firms," draft white paper, https://regmedia.co.uk/2018/07/30/warner_social_media_proposal.pdf.

7. Ellen J. Langer, "The Illusion of Control," *Journal of Personality and Social Psychology* 32, no. 2 (1975): 311–328.

8. Sarah Spiekermann, Bettina Berendt, and Jens Grossklags, "E-Privacy in 2nd Generation E-Commerce: Privacy Preferences versus Actual Behavior," abstract, *SSRN*, February 20, 2009, https://ssrn.com/abstract=761107.

9. Constantine Sedikides, W. Keith Campbell, Glenn Reeder, and Andrew Elliot, "The Relationship Closeness Induction Task," *Representative Research in Social Psychology* 23 (January 1999): 1–4.

10. James W. Pennebaker, "Telling Stories: The Health Benefits of Narrative," *Literature and Medicine* 19, no. 1 (2000): 3–18; Michael Slepian and Edythe Moulton-Tetlock, "Confiding Secrets and Well-Being," preprint submitted April 6, 2018, doi:10.31234/osf.io/dta8n.

11. Diana I. Tamir and Jason P. Mitchell, "Intrinsic Value of Self-Disclosure," *Proceedings of the National Academy of Sciences* 109, no. 21 (May 2012): 8038–8043.

12. Leslie K. John, Alessandro Acquisti, and George Loewenstein, "Strangers on a Plane: Context-Dependent Willingness to Divulge Sensitive Information," *Journal of Consumer Research* 37, no. 5 (February 2011): 858–873.

13. Aleecia M. McDonald and Lorrie Faith Cranor, "The Cost of Reading Privacy Policies," *I/S: A Journal of Law and Policy for the Information Society* 4, no. 3 (2008): 543–568.

Adapted from content posted on hbr.org, October 5, 2018 (product #BG1805).

2

WHY IT'S A BAD IDEA TO LET A FEW TECH COMPANIES MONOPOLIZE OUR DATA

by Maurice E. Stucke

t's no good fighting an election campaign on the facts," Cambridge Analytica's managing director told an undercover reporter, "because actually it's all about emotion." To target U.S. voters and appeal to their hopes, neuroses, and fears, the political consulting firm needed to train its algorithm to predict and map personality traits. That required lots of personal data. So, to build these psychographic profiles, Cambridge Analytica enlisted a Cambridge University professor, whose app collected data on 50 million Facebook users and their friends. Facebook, at that time, allowed app developers to collect this personal data. Facebook argued that Cambridge Analytica and the professor violated its data polices. But this was not the first time its policies were violated. Nor is it likely to be the last.

This scandal came on the heels of Russia's using Facebook, Google, and Twitter "to sow discord in the U.S. political system, including the 2016 U.S. presidential election." It heightened concerns over today's tech giants and the influence they have.

That influence comes in part from data. Facebook, Google, Amazon, and similar companies are "dataopolies." By that I mean companies that control a key platform that, like a coral reef, attracts to its ecosystem users, sellers, advertisers, software developers, app developers, and accessory makers. Apple and Google, for example, each control a popular mobile phone operating system platform (and key apps on that platform), Amazon controls the largest online merchant platform, and Facebook controls the largest social network platform. A significant *volume* and *variety* of personal data flows through their leading platforms. The *velocity* in acquiring and exploiting this personal data can help these companies obtain significant market power. Is it okay for a few firms to possess so much data and thereby wield so much power? In the United States, at least, antitrust officials so far seem ambivalent about these data-opolies. They're free, the thinking goes, so what's the harm? But that reasoning is misguided. Data-opolies pose tremendous risks for consumers, workers, competition, and the overall health of our democracy. Here's why.

Why U.S. Antitrust Isn't Worried About Data-Opolies

The European competition authorities brought actions against four data-opolies: Google, Apple, Facebook, and Amazon. The European Commission, for example, fined Google a record €2.42 billion for leveraging its search monopoly to advance its comparative shopping service. The European Commission also preliminarily found Google to have abused its dominant position both with its Android mobile operating system and with AdSense. Facebook, Germany's competition agency preliminarily found, abused its dominant position "by making the use of its social network conditional on its being allowed to limitlessly amass every kind of data generated by using third-party websites and merge it with the user's Facebook account."

We will likely see more fines and other remedies in the next few years from the Europeans. But in the United States, the data-opolies have largely escaped antitrust scrutiny, under both the Barack Obama and the George W. Bush administrations. Notably, while the European Commission found Google's search bias to be anticompetitive, the U.S. Federal Trade Commission did not. From 2000 onward, the Department of Justice brought only one monopolization case in total, against anyone. (In contrast, the DOJ, between 1970 and 1972, brought 39 civil and 3 criminal cases against monopolies and oligopolies.)

The head of the Department of Justice's Antitrust Division recognized the enforcement gap between the United States and Europe. He noted his agency's "particular concerns in digital markets." But absent "demonstrable harm to competition and consumers," the DOJ is "reluctant to impose special duties on digital platforms, out of [its] concern that special duties might stifle the very innovation that has created dynamic competition for the benefit of consumers."

So the divergence in antitrust enforcement may reflect differences over these data-opolies' perceived harms.

Ordinarily the harm from monopolies is higher prices, less output, or reduced quality. It superficially appears that data-opolies pose little, if any, risk of these harms. Unlike some pharmaceutical companies, data-opolies do not charge consumers exorbitant prices. Most of Google's and Facebook's consumer products are ostensibly "free." The data-opolies' scale can also mean higher-quality products. The more people use a particular search engine, the more the search engine's algorithm can learn users' preferences, and the more relevant the search results will likely be, which in turn will likely attract others to the search engine, and the positive feedback continues.

As Robert Bork argues, there "is no coherent case for monopolization because a search engine, like Google, is free to consumers and they can switch to an alternative search engine with a click."

How Data-Opolies Harm

But higher prices are not the only way for powerful companies to harm their consumers or the rest of society. Upon closer examination, we see that data-opolies can pose at least eight potential harms.

Lower-quality products with less privacy

Companies, antitrust authorities increasingly recognize, can compete on privacy and protecting data. But without competition, data-opolies face less pressure. They can depress privacy protection *below* competitive levels and collect personal data *above* competitive levels. The collection of too much personal data can be the equivalent of charging an excessive price.

Data-opolies can also fail to disclose *what* data they collect and *how* they will use the data. They face little competitive pressure to change their opaque privacy policies. Even if a data-opoly improves its privacy statement, so what? The current notice-and-consent regime is meaningless when there are no viable competitive alternatives and the bargaining power is so unequal.

Surveillance and security risks

In a monopolized market, personal data is concentrated in a few firms. Consumers have limited outside options that offer better privacy protection. This raises additional risks, including:

- **Government capture.** The fewer the firms controlling the personal data, the greater the potential risk that a government will capture the firm. Companies need things from government; governments often want access to data. When there are only a few firms, this can increase the likelihood of companies secretly cooperating with the government to provide access to data. China, for example, relies on its data-opolies to better monitor its population.

- **Covert surveillance.** Even if the government cannot capture a data-opoly, its rich data trove increases a government's incentive to circumvent the data-opoly's privacy protections to tap into the personal data. Even if the government can't strike a deal to access the data directly, it may be able to do so covertly.

- **Implications of a data policy violation or security breach.** Data-opolies have greater incentives to prevent a breach than do typical firms. But with more personal data concentrated in fewer companies, hackers, marketers, and political consultants, among others, have even greater incentives to find ways to circumvent or breach the dominant firm's security measures. The concentration of data means that if one of them is breached, the harm done could be orders of magnitude greater than with a normal company. While consumers may be outraged, a dominant firm has less reason to worry about consumers' switching to rivals.

Wealth transfer to data-opolies

Even when their products and services are ostensibly "free," data-opolies can extract significant wealth in several ways that they otherwise couldn't in a competitive market.

First, data-opolies can extract wealth by getting personal data without having to pay the data's fair market value. The personal data collected may be worth far more than the cost of providing the free service. The fact that the service is free does not mean we are fairly compensated for our data. Thus, data-opolies have a strong economic incentive to maintain the status quo, in which users, as *MIT Technology Review* put it, "have little idea how much personal data they have provided, how it is used, and what it is worth." If the public knew, and if they had viable alternatives, they might hold out for compensation.

Second, something similar can happen with the content users create. Data-opolies can extract wealth by getting creative content from users for free. In a competitive market, users could conceivably demand compensation not only for their data but also their contributions to

YouTube and Facebook. With no viable alternatives, they cannot.

Third, data-opolies can extract wealth from sellers upstream. One example is when data-opolies scrape valuable content from photographers, authors, musicians, and others' websites and post it on their own platform. In this case, the wealth of the data-opolies comes at the expense of other businesses in their value chain.

Fourth, data-opolies can extract our wealth indirectly, when their higher advertising fees are passed along in the prices for the advertised goods and services. If the data-opolies had more competitors for their advertising services, ads could cost even less—and therefore so might the products being advertised.

Finally, data-opolies can extract wealth from both sellers upstream and consumers downstream by facilitating or engaging in *behavioral discrimination*, a form of price discrimination based on past behavior—such as internet browsing history. Data-opolies can use the personal data to get people to buy things they did not necessarily want at the highest price they are willing to pay.

As data-opolies expand their platforms to digital personal assistants, the Internet of Things, and smart technologies, the concern is that their data advantage will increase their competitive advantage and market power. As a result, the data-opolies' monopoly profits will likely increase, at our expense.

Loss of trust

Market economies rely on trust. For online markets to deliver their benefits, people must trust firms and their use of personal data. But as technology evolves and more personal data is collected, we are increasingly aware that a few powerful firms are using our personal information for their benefit, not ours. When data-opolies degrade privacy protections below competitive levels, some consumers will choose "to [not] share their data, to limit their data sharing with companies, or even to lie when providing information," as the U. K. Competition and Markets Authority put it. Consumers may forgo the data-opolies' services, which they otherwise would have used if privacy competition were robust. This loss would represent what economists call a deadweight welfare loss. In other words, as distrust increases, society overall becomes worse off.

Significant costs on third parties

Additionally, data-opolies that control a key platform, like a mobile phone operating system, can cheaply exclude rivals by:

- steering users and advertisers to their own products and services to the detriment of rival sellers on the platform (and contrary to consumers' wishes)

- degrading an independent app's functionality

- reducing traffic to an independent app by making it harder to find via its search engine or in its app store

Data-opolies can also impose costs on companies seeking to protect our privacy interests. My book with Ariel Ezrachi, *Virtual Competition*, discusses, for example, Google's kicking the privacy app Disconnect out of its Android app store.

Less innovation in markets dominated by data-opolies

Data-opolies can chill innovation with a weapon that earlier monopolies lacked. Allen Grunes and I call it the "now-casting radar." Our book *Big Data and Competition Policy* explores how some platforms have a relative advantage in accessing and analyzing data to discern consumer trends well before others. Data-opolies can use their relative advantage to see what products or services are becoming more popular. With their now-casting radar, data-opolies can acquire or squelch these nascent competitive threats.

Social and moral concerns

Historically, antitrust has also been concerned with how monopolies can hinder individual autonomy. Data-opolies can also hurt individual autonomy. To start with, they can direct (and limit) opportunities for startups that subsist on their super platform. This includes third-party sellers that rely on Amazon's platform to reach consumers, newspapers and journalists who depend on Facebook and Google to reach younger readers, and as the European Commission's Google Shopping Case explores, companies that depend on traffic from Google's search engine.

But the autonomy concerns go beyond the constellation of app developers, sellers, journalists, musicians, writers, photographers, and artists dependent on the data-opoly to reach users. Every individual's autonomy is at stake. In January, the hedge fund Jana Partners joined the California State Teachers' Retirement System pension fund to demand that Apple do more to address the effects of its devices on children. As the *Economist* noted, "You know you are in trouble if a Wall Street firm is lecturing you about morality." The concern is that the data-opolies' products are purposefully addictive and thereby eroding individuals' ability to make free choices.

There is an interesting counterargument that's worth noting, based on the interplay between monopoly power and competition. On the one hand, in monopolized markets, consumers have fewer competitive options, and arguably, there is less need to addict them. On the other hand, data-opolies like Facebook and Google, even without significant rivals, can increase profits by increasing our engagement with their products. Data-opolies can have an incentive to exploit behavioral biases and imperfect willpower to addict users—whether watching YouTube videos or posting on Instagram.

Political concerns

Economic power often translates into political power. Unlike earlier monopolies, data-opolies, given how they interact with individuals, possess a more powerful tool: the ability to affect the public debate and our perception of right and wrong.

Many people now receive their news from social media platforms. But the news isn't just passively transmitted. Data-opolies can influence how we feel and think. Facebook, for example, in an "emotional contagion" study, manipulated 689,003 users' emotions by altering their news feed. Other risks of this sort include:

- **Bias.** In filtering the information we receive based on our preferences, data-opolies can reduce the viewpoints we receive, thereby leading to echo chambers and filter bubbles.

- **Censorship.** Data-opolies, through their platform, can control or block content that users receive and enforce governmental censorship of political or religious information.

- **Manipulation.** Data-opolies can promote stories that further their particular business or political interests instead of their relevance or quality.

Limiting the Power of Data-Opolies

Upon closer examination, data-opolies can actually be *more* dangerous than traditional monopolies. They can affect not only our wallets but our privacy, autonomy, democracy, and well-being.

Markets dominated by these data-opolies will not necessarily self-correct. Network effects, high switching costs for consumers (given the lack of data portability and user rights over their data), and weak privacy protection help data-opolies maintain their dominance.

Luckily, global antitrust enforcement can help. The Ronald Reagan administration, in espousing the then-popular Chicago school of economics beliefs, discounted concerns over monopolies. The Supreme Court, relying on faulty economic reasoning, surmised that charging monopoly prices was "an important element of the free market system." With the rise of a progressive, antimonopoly New Brandeis school, the pendulum is swinging the other way. Given the emergence of data-opolies, this is a welcome change.

Nonetheless, global antitrust enforcement, while a necessary tool to deter these harms, is not sufficient. Antitrust enforcers must coordinate with privacy and consumer protection officials to ensure that the conditions for effective privacy competition and an inclusive economy are in place.

TAKEAWAYS

Many tech giants are "data-opolies." The volume, variety, and velocity of personal data flows through these ecosystems help these companies gain significant market power. They control key platforms that attract users, sellers, advertisers, software developers, app developers, and accessory makers to their ecosystems.

✓ Concentrating personal data in fewer firms increases surveillance and security risks. Data-opolies can negatively affect not only consumers' wallets but their privacy, autonomy, democracy, and well-being.

✓ Even though most products and services the data-opolies provide are "free," these companies can extract significant wealth using a variety of means, including personal data collection, appropriating user-created content, and selling data to other vendors.

✓ Allowing data-opolies to go unchecked introduces potential harms including security risks, declining innovation, and social, moral, and political concerns.

Adapted from "Here Are All the Reasons It's a Bad Idea to Let a Few Tech Companies Monopolize Our Data" on hbr.org, March 27, 2018 (product #H048R4).

PRIVACY AND CYBERSECURITY ARE CONVERGING

Here's Why That Matters for People and for Companies

by Andrew Burt

P rivacy issues have dominated headlines in recent years. These events are symptoms of larger, profound shifts in the world of data privacy and security that have major implications for how organizations think about and manage both.

So what exactly is changing?

Put simply, privacy and security are converging, thanks to the rise of big data and machine learning. What was once an abstract concept designed to protect expectations about our own data is now becoming more concrete, and more critical—on par with the threat of adversaries accessing our data without authorization.

More specifically, the threat of *unauthorized access* to our data used to pose the biggest danger to our digital selves—that was a world in which we worried about intruders attempting to get at data we wanted private. And it was a world in which privacy and security were largely separate functions, where privacy took a back seat to the more tangible concerns over security. Today, however, the biggest risk to our privacy and our security has become the threat of *unintended inferences*, due to the power of increasingly widespread machine learning techniques. Once we generate data, anyone who possesses enough of it can be a threat, posing new dangers to both our privacy and our security.

These inferences may, for example, threaten our anonymity—like when a group of researchers used machine learning techniques to identify authorship of written text based simply on patterns in language.[1] (Similar techniques have been used to identify software developers based simply on the code they've written.[2])

These inferences might reveal information about our political leanings—like when researchers used the prevalence of certain types of cars in Google's Street View image database to determine local political affiliations.[3] Or these inferences might also indicate intimate details about our health—like when researchers used online search history to detect neurodegenerative disorders such as Alzheimer's.[4]

So what does a world look like when privacy and security are focused on preventing the same harms?

To start with, privacy will no longer be the merely immaterial or political concept it once was. Instead, privacy will begin to have substantial impacts on businesses' bottom lines—something we began to see in 2018. Facebook, for example, lost a whopping $119 billion in market capitalization in the wake of the Cambridge Analytica scandal because of concerns over privacy. Polls show that consumers are increasingly concerned about privacy issues. And governments around the world are reacting with new privacy legislation of their own.

Within organizations, this convergence also means that the once-clear line between privacy and security teams is beginning to blur—a trend that businesses in general, and security and privacy practitioners in particular, should embrace. From a practical perspective, this means that legal and privacy personnel will become more technical, and technical personnel will become more familiar with legal and compliance mandates. The idea of two distinct teams, operating independently of each other, will become a relic of the past.

And this means individuals and governments alike should no longer expect consent to play a meaningful role in protecting our privacy. Because the threat of unintended inferences reduces our ability to understand the value of our data, our expectations about our privacy—and therefore what we can meaningfully consent to—are becoming less consequential. Being *surprised* at the nature of the violation, in short, will become an inherent feature of future privacy and security harms.

This is precisely why the recent string of massive data breaches, from the Marriott breach that impacted 500 million guests to the Yahoo breach that affected 3 billion users, is so troubling. The problem isn't simply that unauthorized intruders accessed these records at a single point in time; the problem is all the unforeseen uses and all the intimate inferences that this volume of data can generate going forward. It is for this reason that legal scholars such as Oxford's Sandra Wachter are now proposing legal constraints around the ability to perform this type of pattern recognition at all.[5]

Once described by Supreme Court justice Louis Brandeis as "the right to be let alone," privacy is now best described as the ability to control data we cannot stop generating, giving rise to inferences we can't predict.

And because we create more and more data every day—an estimated 2.5 quintillion bytes of it—these issues will only become more pressing over time.

Thanks to the rise of big data and machine learning, privacy and security are converging. The largest threat is no longer unauthorized access to our data—it is the unintended, uncannily accurate inferences made by algorithms that are able to sift through and combine multiple sets of data:

✓ Consumers and government are taking note, by abandoning platforms they can't trust and introducing new privacy legislation.

✓ For organizations, this means security and privacy teams will have to work together more closely; legal and privacy personnel will become more technical, and technical personnel will become more familiar with legal and compliance mandates.

✓ For individuals and governments, this means consent will no longer play a meaningful role in protecting privacy.

NOTES

1. Arvind Narayanan et al., "On the Feasibility of Internet-Scale Author Identification," 2012 IEEE Symposium on Security and Privacy, May 2012, https://ieeexplore.ieee.org/document/6234420 /authors#authors.

2. Aylin Caliskan et al., "When Coding Style Survives Compilation: De-anonymizing Programmers from Executable Binaries," Cornell University working paper, December 18, 2017, https://arxiv .org/abs/1512.08546.

3. Timnit Gebru et al., "Using Deep Learning and Google Street View to Estimate the Demographic Makeup of the US," *PNAS* 114, no. 50 (2017): 13108–13113.

4. Ryen W. White, P. Murali Doraiswamy, and Eric Horvitz, "Detecting Neurodegenerative Disorders from Web Search Signals," *Nature*, April 23, 2018, https://www.nature.com/articles/s41746-018 -0016-6.

5. Sandra Wachter and Brent Mittelstadt, "A Right to Reasonable Inferences: Re-Thinking Data Protection Law in the Age of Big Data and AI," *Columbia Business Law Review*, September 13, 2018, https://papers.ssrn.com/sol3/papers.cfm?abstract_id=3248829.

Adapted from content posted on hbr.org, January 3, 2019 (product #H04PY8).

A STRONG PRIVACY POLICY CAN SAVE YOUR COMPANY MILLIONS

by Kelly D. Martin, Abhishek Borah, and Robert W. Palmatier

Cyberattacks are on the rise, with over 1,000 data breaches occurring at U.S. organizations in 2016 alone, most often through hacking or external theft. And it isn't only violated firms that are hurt by these incidents. Studying hundreds of data breaches, our research has found that data breaches sometimes harm a firm's close rivals (because of spillover effects) but sometimes help them (because of competitive effects). We also found that a good corporate privacy policy can shield firms from the financial harm posed by a data breach—by offering customers transparency and control over their personal information—while a flawed policy can exacerbate the problems caused by a breach. This is the first evidence to show that a firm's close rivals are directly, financially affected by its data breach, and our research offers actionable solutions that could save some companies hundreds of millions of dollars.

Our research shows that sometimes a breach creates spillover, in which investors perceive a guilt-by-association effect that harms the breached firm's close rivals. For an example of competitor harm due to these spillover effects, consider the Nvidia data breach, which affected 400,000 user accounts. Its rival Advanced Micro Devices (AMD) lost about $48 million on the event day (1.4% drop in stock price) from the spillover effects of Nvidia's breach, controlling for overall market effects. That is, when removing from our analyses all other events that could have influenced AMD's stock drop, such as dividend declarations, contract signings, earnings information, or mergers and

---

Editor's note: Every ranking or index is just one way to analyze and compare companies or places, based on a specific methodology and data set. At HBR, we believe that a well-designed index can provide useful insights, even though by definition it is a snapshot of a bigger picture. We always urge you to read the methodology carefully.

acquisitions, we find clear and significant harm to AMD from Nvidia's data breach.

In fact, the spillover effects across our sample led to a drop in stock price that averaged more than $8 million in losses for rival firms where no such data breach occurred. Our results show the financial hit to these rivals' stock prices can be detected for several days after the data breach before eventually stabilizing.

Yet a breach can sometimes help a close rival, creating beneficial competitive effects. Consider the massive Anthem data breach, which affected as many as 80 million customers. The high severity of this breach led rival Aetna to gain about $745 million (2.2% increase in stock prices) on the event day, due to competitive effects, again controlling for overall market effects. A data breach of this type and scale makes investors worry about customers defecting en masse to competitors, thus providing a boost to a close competitor's stock price.

Our research shows that the severity of, or number of customers affected by, a breach is a key to understanding whether close rivals will be harmed or helped by their competitor's bad fortune. As the number of customers harmed by the breach increases, stock market effects for the firm's rivals go from negative to positive, as competitive effects become more dominant. This suggests that smaller breaches signal that others in the industry may also be vulnerable to hacking. However, large data breaches create the impression that the breached firm is in a unique amount of trouble. Our research shows that in large data breaches, customers' desire to leave the breached firm increased. Expected switching behavior ultimately benefits the breached firm's competitors, as captured in their stock returns.

The good news is that firms are not powerless against these data breach effects. There are actionable strategies they can use to protect or inoculate themselves from their own or a rival's breach. Using studies querying hundreds of customers whom we recruited on Amazon Mechanical Turk, coupled with stock data analysis of hundreds of companies over 10 years, our research finds that firms can protect themselves from data breach harm by implementing two important privacy-focused practices that benefit customers.

First, they can clearly explain to customers how they are using and sharing their data. Transparent privacy practices tell customers what specific information companies capture (such as IP address and search history) and how they use it (for example, using in promotions or selling to third parties). Second, firms can give customers ample control over the use and sharing of their data. Control is endowed through giving customers opportunities to opt out of the firm's data practices (promotions, sharing with partners, selling). Together, these measures were perceived to effectively empower customers, giving them greater knowledge and the ability to have a say in business practices. (See the sidebar "Why Study Privacy Policies?")

Why Study Privacy Policies?

Although companies can provide transparency and control through various customer communications, the formalized and codified way they do this is privacy policies. These policies are important customer communication tools because the firm has legally agreed to abide by them. Regardless of what a company might message about data privacy in other ways, what is put into practice is formally documented in the privacy policy. When customers are in doubt about their personal information, company messaging commonly refers them to the privacy policy. A review of data privacy research in marketing found that customers do, in fact, have a good idea of a firm's data practices as captured in a firm's privacy policy—even if they don't read the privacy policy. Because privacy policies simply document all company privacy practices, customers who are familiar with a given company and its approach to privacy have a highly accurate sense of what is in the policy. Again, our research with hundreds of customers confirmed this.

When a firm had transparent privacy practices, customers in our studies felt they had the knowledge to make an informed decision about sharing their personal data. When a firm's privacy practices offered control, customers knew they had the ability to change their preferences about what information they shared and how. In our studies, customers did not punish breached firms that provided both transparency and control. Empowered customers are more willing to share information and are more forgiving of data privacy breaches, remaining loyal after the fact, as we learned. Customers of firms that offer high transparency and control reported feeling less violated by big data practices, attested to being more trusting, provided more-accurate data to the firm, and were more likely to generate positive word of mouth.

Firms with relatively high transparency and control also were buffered from stock price damage during data breaches, either their own or rivals'. Yet only about 10% of *Fortune* 500 firms fit this profile.

To study how a firm implements practices that provide transparency and control, we looked at the documented ways in which companies explain their approach to customer data privacy. Our research team combed through the privacy policies of all *Fortune* 100 firms to study their transparency and control and from that understand how protected the firms were from the negative effects of data breaches.

Our findings show that some firms provide high levels of data transparency and control and would be protected from data breaches. (See our ranking in figure 4-1.) Top-ranked firms such as Costco, Verizon, and HP would be

FIGURE 4-1

How good are the *Fortune* 100's privacy policies?

A ranking of how transparent each company's policy is, and how much control it gives customers.

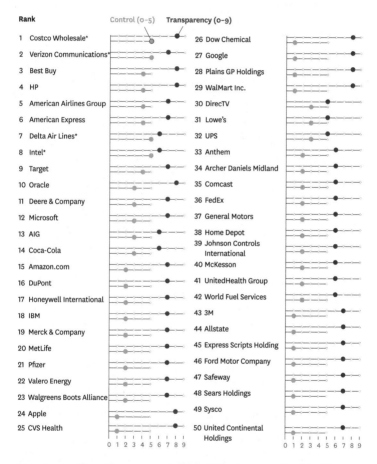

Rank		Control (0-5)	Transparency (0-9)
1	Costco Wholesale*		
2	Verizon Communications*		
3	Best Buy		
4	HP		
5	American Airlines Group		
6	American Express		
7	Delta Air Lines*		
8	Intel*		
9	Target		
10	Oracle		
11	Deere & Company		
12	Microsoft		
13	AIG		
14	Coca-Cola		
15	Amazon.com		
16	DuPont		
17	Honeywell International		
18	IBM		
19	Merck & Company		
20	MetLife		
21	Pfizer		
22	Valero Energy		
23	Walgreens Boots Alliance		
24	Apple		
25	CVS Health		

26	Dow Chemical
27	Google
28	Plains GP Holdings
29	WalMart Inc.
30	DirecTV
31	Lowe's
32	UPS
33	Anthem
34	Archer Daniels Midland
35	Comcast
36	FedEx
37	General Motors
38	Home Depot
39	Johnson Controls International
40	McKesson
41	UnitedHealth Group
42	World Fuel Services
43	3M
44	Allstate
45	Express Scripts Holding
46	Ford Motor Company
47	Safeway
48	Sears Holdings
49	Sysco
50	United Continental Holdings

*The privacy policies of these companies offer additional opt outs that did not factor into our ranking.

(Continued)

FIGURE 4-1 *(continued)*

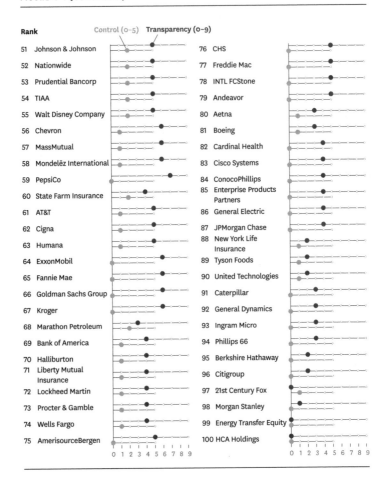

shielded from spillover effects if a close competitor experienced a data breach. These firms clearly state what information they capture and how they capture it while offering their customers substantial control over that information's sharing and use.

On the other end of the ranking are firms such as Citigroup, Morgan Stanley, and HCA Holdings. In 2011 Citigroup experienced a data breach of 146,000 customer records and suffered a $1.3 billion stock value loss. According to our analysis, if Citigroup had embraced practices of high transparency and high control, it would have suffered a loss of only about $16 million in stock value. That is, Citigroup might have saved about $820 million had it simply offered its customers high transparency and control. In response to this breach, Citigroup spent $250 million on cybersecurity systems and hired an additional 1,000 IT professionals. Yet our coding of its practices reveals that, as recently as 2016, Citi still was not providing high levels of transparency and control. Thus, while its enhanced IT safeguards may be sound, our research shows the company remains at risk should a competitor suffer a breach. (See the sidebar "Company Ranking Methodology.")

Looking across the ranking, other firms appear to offer one of these aspects to customers. For example, some firms provide transparency but fail to give customers the ability to act on this information (low control). In our research, this approach was poorly received by customers.

Firms that neither tell customers how their data is used nor offer any control are at the greatest risk of financial harm. Our privacy analysis showed that an overwhelming 80% of *Fortune* 500 firms fall into this category. In our

Company Ranking Methodology

We created transparency and control variables with procedures that employed a mix of automation and manual coding of companies' actual privacy policies.

We first captured all the relevant URLs pertaining to firms' privacy policies that were in effect on January 1, 2016. We developed a Python code that visited all valid snapshots of each *Fortune* 500 firm's privacy policy to extract that closest to our date of interest. To ensure the correct URLs were downloaded and parsed, a random 5% of the URLs were manually checked to find if there were errors in the code, and the errors were corrected. We then resampled the URLs and found no errors. After obtaining the privacy policies, we manually coded transparency and control variables by carefully reading each privacy policy and using a coding schema to create count scores for transparency and control. For the variables that required coding of events, we followed standard procedures for textual coding.

For the textual coding procedure, we employed two research assistants who were blind to the study hypothesis. Before coding the privacy policies, the two were separately trained in the coding scheme on a sample of privacy policies that were not part of the final sample. One of us checked

Company Ranking Methodology

to ensure the research assistants understood the coding scheme. After obtaining all the privacy policies, each research assistant independently coded them. Agreement between the two research assistants on the coding was greater than 85%. Disagreements in coding were resolved through discussion with us.

For the transparency variable, we used a count of the dummy variables across multiple elements of the privacy policy that signal openness and willingness to provide information to customers. Specifically, we coded whether the firm (1) explains its opt-out policy, (2) explains how it captures data, (3) explains how it uses data, (4) explains its use of tracking tools, (5) explains the value customers receive from providing their information, (6) explains its data sharing with third parties, (7) explains its data encryption practices, (8) provides contact information for privacy requests, and (9) discusses protections if data is compromised. If a firm's privacy policy had all nine characteristics, the policy earned a transparency score of nine.

To create the control variable, we counted the number of opt-out choices in the firm's privacy policy. Specifically, we

(Continued)

coded whether the customer can opt out of (1) marketing communications, (2) saving data usage (for example, search history), (3) storing personal information (for example, credit card number), (4) sharing data with third parties, and (5) tracking. If a firm's privacy policy had all five characteristics, the policy earned a control score of five. Note that we also counted opt outs that were not on this list but were featured as part of the firm's privacy policy. Four firms included additional data collection or data-use opt outs beyond our five characteristics. These were firm-specific opt outs that enabled greater customer control but did not warrant separate opt-out categories for the entire sample of firms.

To create our ranking, we compiled the summed scores of transparency and control for all firms. Firms that had identical scores on both dimensions appear alphabetically in the ranking.

study, firms that failed to explain their data privacy practices had a drop in stock price 1.5 times larger than firms with high transparency, while firms that provided customers high control had no significant change in their stock price after a data breach.

Ultimately, firms can use data privacy practices to protect themselves from the spillover effects of competitors' privacy failures, but their efforts to do so need to be meaningful. They must clearly explain to customers the ways in which they will access, use, share, and protect customer information, and it must go hand in hand with giving customers control over these data uses. Failure to do so leaves a firm susceptible to risk from multiple harms.

TAKEAWAYS

Data breaches can create significant ripples beyond the violated firm, affecting the valuation of other companies in the industry. But firms are not powerless against these effects.

✓ To protect themselves from the effects of their own or a rival's breach, companies can implement two privacy-focused practices that also benefit customers.

- Clearly explain to customers how they are using and sharing their data.

- Give customers control over the use and sharing of their data (including opportunities to opt out).

✓ Research shows that when customers know they have the ability to change their data-sharing preferences they're more willing to share information and are more forgiving of data privacy breaches.

Adapted from "Research: A Strong Privacy Policy Can Save Your Company Millions" on hbr.org, February 15, 2018 (product #H0465E).

DO YOU CARE ABOUT PRIVACY AS MUCH AS YOUR CUSTOMERS DO?

by Thomas C. Redman and Robert M. Waitman

Companies have had little compelling reason to embed privacy considerations deeply into their larger business strategies. Consumers say they care about privacy, but few have placed any real value on protecting their data. While many privacy laws call for severe penalties, it appears that actual fines will be considerably lower and only the worst offenders will be affected. The costs to fully meet all privacy requirements can also be quite high for most companies.

On the other side of the ledger, sharing consumer data or using it in targeted marketing campaigns, to train algorithms, and so forth, offers outsize potential. Indeed, *not* exploiting customer data when your competitors are doing so can put you at a significant disadvantage. One sound privacy strategy is to maintain a low profile. Name data protection officers, ask customers for consent (as called for by the European Union General Data Protection Regulation, or GDPR), and provide roughly the same levels of privacy protections as your competitors at the minimum possible cost.

That approach, however, may prove shortsighted. A survey conducted by Cisco of 2,601 adults worldwide examined the actions, not just attitudes, of consumers with respect to their data privacy.[1] (Robert led the work, Tom advised.) The survey reveals an important new group of people—32% of respondents—who said they care about privacy, are willing to act, *and* have done so by switching companies or providers over data or data-sharing policies. We call this group *privacy actives* and, to our best knowledge, this is the first time such a group has been identified.

The notion that significant numbers of privacy actives even exist should raise antennae at all companies. By understanding this unique group of individuals, whose feelings about privacy are multifaceted and complex, companies can shape their own data and customer privacy practices and better engage, retain, and work with these customers.

According to the survey, privacy actives tend to be younger, more affluent, and shop more online—a segment of the population that is especially attractive to most companies. They are more than twice as likely (27% versus 11%) to view themselves as early tech adopters, and they are more frequent users of social media.

Privacy actives see respect for privacy as core to the brands of the companies with which they do business: 90% believe the ways their data is treated reflects how they are treated as customers. Not surprisingly, they also say they will not buy from companies if they don't trust how their data is used.

But the survey also reveals some counterintuitive findings about privacy actives. The Cisco survey presented multiple scenarios involving respondents' levels of comfort with sharing their data in exchange for more personalized products or other benefits. Surprisingly, privacy actives were *more* comfortable with these trade-offs compared with their nonactive counterparts. For instance, when asked if they were willing to provide purchase history in exchange for personalized products and services, 62% of privacy actives were comfortable with the trade-off versus 32% of non–privacy actives. When asked if they were willing to share information from smart home speakers in exchange for health and safety warnings for the entire family, 44% of privacy actives were comfortable versus only 17% of non–privacy actives. Across the board, privacy actives were twice as likely to be comfortable with sharing their information in exchange for a personal or public benefit.

When asked whether they felt they could protect their privacy today, 67% of privacy actives responded that they could (52% of non–privacy actives agreed). But that still leaves a third of privacy actives who do not feel they can protect their own privacy. The chief complaint of this subgroup is that it is too difficult to figure out what companies are doing with their data. It is impossible to evaluate a trade-off when you don't know what data will be used for what purposes. According to the survey, 83% of privacy actives read privacy policies. But even the general notice—"By using this site, you agree to our updated Privacy Policy and Terms of Use"—can be unclear to the average consumer, covering anything from "We only use your data so our website responds more quickly to your requests" to "BEWARE! We track your every move and sell your data every chance we get." A detailed privacy policy or terms-of-use page may be well intentioned, but sorting it out is a lot of work and may not be enough for these important customers.

So how should you put these findings to work?

First, these findings indicate that privacy is as much about customer experience as it is about privacy itself. So get the right people involved. We find it telling that companies routinely seek consumers' feedback regarding their products and services, yet neither one of us can recall ever being asked about privacy. Go directly to your customers to get to know your privacy actives—how many there are, their views on your privacy policies, their openness to your new ideas, and what they view as fair compensation for your use of their data. A good way to start might involve extending current survey vehicles to these questions.

Second, use your newfound knowledge to engage privacy actives as you explore new ways to use data. They are simultaneously more receptive to new ideas that will help you build your business and more likely to raise the caution flags that will keep you from making big mistakes. And keep in mind that, as you're engaging these customers, another 29% are concerned about privacy and are willing to act but haven't done so yet—they're only one step away from becoming privacy actives themselves. Consider reaching out to these folks now, before they make a change.

Third, address the transparency gap that privacy actives have called out. Simplify and shorten your privacy policies so people can access, read, and understand them quickly—in no more than two minutes. Clarify the compensation customers and users may expect in exchange for their data, whether in money, discounts, or services, and make it easier to opt in or out.

Finally, while we expect the privacy landscape to change rapidly and chaotically over the next several years, now is a good time to think long term. Years ago, when Tom worked at Bell Labs, an unknown prognosticator noted that "privacy will be to the Information Age as product safety was to the Industrial Age." This individual observed that, over time, societies came to expect companies to produce safe products. Both legal and market pressures came to bear. In some cases, these protections may have gone too far—is it really necessary to warn coffee drinkers, "Caution, contents may be hot"? But right or wrong, that is how society voted.

So ask yourself these questions: Do you think there is wisdom in the prediction? Do you have a different one? How do you want to position your company and its brand with respect to privacy over the long term? As you puzzle through these questions, we think you will see many opportunities in embracing data privacy.

Meet a new type of consumer: privacy actives. These people say they care about their privacy, are willing to act, *and* have demonstrated this by taking concrete action—deleting accounts, letting subscriptions lapse, doing business elsewhere—over data or data-sharing policies. To earn the trust and the business of privacy actives, your organization needs to:

✓ Recognize that privacy is as much about customer experience as it is about privacy itself.

✓ Modify surveys you already distribute to get customers' input about privacy policies and fair use of their data.

✓ Engage your privacy actives to help you explore new ways to use data. They'll help you build your business, and they'll raise red flags before you make big mistakes.

✓ Simplify and shorten your privacy policies; ideally, make them something users can read in
under two minutes. Clarify what compensation
consumers may expect in exchange for their data,
whether it's money or an easy way to opt out.

NOTE

1. Cisco, *Consumer Privacy Survey*, November 2019, https://www
.cisco.com/c/dam/en/us/products/collateral/security/cybersecurity
-series-2019-cps.pdf.

Adapted from content posted on hbr.org, January 28, 2020 (product #H05DVH).

6

HOW TO EXERCISE THE POWER YOU DIDN'T ASK FOR

by Jonathan Zittrain

I used to be largely indifferent to claims about the use of private data for targeted advertising, even as I worried about privacy more generally. How much of an intrusion was it, really, for a merchant to hit me with a banner ad for dog food instead of cat food, since it had reason to believe I owned a dog? And any users who were sensitive about their personal information could just click on a menu and simply opt out of that kind of tracking.

But times have changed.

The digital surveillance economy has ballooned in size and sophistication while keeping most of its day-to-day tracking apparatus out of view. Public reaction has ranged from muted to deeply concerned, with a good portion of those in the concerned camp feeling so overwhelmed by the pervasiveness of their privacy loss that they're more or less reconciled to it. It's long past time not only to worry but to act.

Advertising dog food to dog owners remains innocuous, but pushing payday loans to people identified as being emotionally and financially vulnerable is not. Neither is targeted advertising that is used to *exclude* people. Julia Angwin, Ariana Tobin, and Madeleine Varner found that on Facebook targeting could be used to show housing ads only to white consumers.[1] Narrow targeting can also render long-standing mechanisms for detecting market failure and abuse ineffective: State attorneys general or consumer advocates can't respond to a deceitful ad campaign, for instance, when they don't see it themselves. Uber took this predicament to cartoon villain extremes when, to avoid sting operations by local regulators, it used data collected from the Uber app to figure out who the officials were and then sent fake information about cars in service to their phones.

These are relatively new problems. Originally, our use of information platforms, whether search engines or social media, wasn't tailored much to anything about us, except through our own direct choices. Your search results for the query "Are vaccinations safe?" would be the same as mine or, for a term like *pizza*, varied in a straightforward way, such as by location, offering up nearby restaurants. If you didn't like what you got, the absence of tailoring suggested that the search platform wasn't to blame; you simply were seeing a window on the web at large. For a long time that was a credible, even desirable, position for content aggregators to take. And for the most part they themselves weren't always good at predicting what their own platforms would offer up. It was a roulette wheel, removed from any human agent's shaping.

Today that's not true. The digital world has gone from pull to push: Instead of actively searching for specific things, people read whatever content is in the feeds they see on sites like Facebook and Twitter. And more and more, people get not a range of search results but a single answer from a virtual concierge like Amazon's Alexa. And it may not be long before such concierges rouse themselves to suggest it's time to buy a gift for a friend's birthday (perhaps from a sponsor) or persistently recommend Uber over Lyft when asked to procure a ride (again, thanks to sponsorship).

Is it still fair for search platforms to say, "Don't blame me, blame the web!" if a concierge provides the wrong directions to a location or the wrong drug interaction precautions? While we tend not to hold Google and Bing responsible for the accuracy of every link they return on a search, the case may be different when platforms actively pluck out only one answer to a question—or answer a question that wasn't even asked.

We've also moved to a world where online news feeds—and in some cases concierges' answers to questions—are aggressively manipulated by third parties trying to gain exposure for their messages. There's great concern about what happens when those messages are propaganda—that is, false and offered in bad faith, often obscuring their origins. Elections can be swayed, and people physically hurt, by lies. Should the platforms be in the business of deciding what's true or not, the way that newspapers are? Or does that open the door to content control by a handful of corporate parties—after all, Facebook has access to far more eyeballs than a single newspaper has ever had—or by the governments that regulate them?

Companies can no longer sit this out, much as they'd like to. As platforms provide highly curated and often single responses to consumers' queries, they're likely to face heated questions—and perhaps regulatory scrutiny—about whom they're favoring or disfavoring. They can't just shrug and point to a "neutral" algorithm when asked why their results are the way they are. That abdication of responsibility has led to abuse by sophisticated and well-funded propagandists, who often build Astroturf campaigns that are meant to look as if they're grassroots.

So what should mediating platforms do?

An answer lies in recognizing that today's issues with surveillance and targeting stem from habit and misplaced trust. People share information about themselves without realizing it and are unaware of how it gets used, passed on, and sold. But the remedy of allowing them to opt out of data collection leads to decision fatigue for users, who can articulate few specific preferences about data practices and simply wish not to be taken advantage of.

Restaurants must meet minimum standards for cleanliness, or (ideally) they'll be shut down. We don't ask the public to research food safety before grabbing a bite and then to opt out of the dubious dining establishments. No one would rue being deprived of the choice to eat food contaminated with salmonella. Similar intervention is needed in the digital universe.

Of course, best practices for the use of personal information online aren't nearly as clear-cut as those for restaurant cleanliness. After all, much of the personalization that results from online surveillance is truly valued by customers. That's why we should turn to a different kind of relationship for inspiration: one in which the person gathering and using information is a skilled, hired professional helping the person whose data is in play. That is the context of interactions between doctors and patients, lawyers and clients, and certified financial planners and investors.

Yale Law School's Jack Balkin has invoked these examples and proposed that today's online platforms become "information fiduciaries." We are among a number of academics who have been working with policy makers and internet companies to map out what sorts of duties a responsible platform could embrace. We've found that our proposal has bipartisan appeal in Congress, because it protects consumers and corrects a clear market failure without the need for heavy-handed government intervention.

Fiduciary has a legalese ring to it, but it's a longstanding, commonsense notion. The key characteristic of fiduciaries is loyalty: They must act in their charges' best interests and, when conflicts arise, must put their charges' interests above their own. That makes them trustworthy. Like doctors, lawyers, and financial advisers, social media platforms and their concierges are given sensitive information by their users, and those users expect a fair shake— whether they're trying to find out what's going on in the world or how to get somewhere or do something.

A fiduciary duty wouldn't broadly rule out targeted advertising—dog owners would still get dog food ads— but it would preclude predatory advertising, like promotions for payday loans. It would also prevent data from being used for purposes unrelated to the expectations of the people who shared it, as happened with the "personality quiz" survey results that were later used to psychometrically profile voters and then attempt to sway their political opinions.

This approach would eliminate the need to judge good from bad content, because it would let platforms make decisions based on what their users want, rather than on what society wants for them. Most users want the truth and should be offered it; others may not value accuracy and may prefer colorful and highly opinionated content instead—and when they do, they should get it, perhaps labeled as such. Aggregators like Google News and Facebook are already starting to make such determinations about what to include as "news" and what counts as "everything else." It may well be that an already-skeptical public only digs in further when these giants offer their judgments, but well-grounded tools could also inform journalists and help prevent propaganda posted on Facebook from spreading into news outlets.

More generally, the fiduciary approach would bring some coherence to the piecemeal privacy protections that have emerged over the years. The right to know what data has been collected about you, the right to ask that it be corrected or purged, and the right to withhold certain data entirely all jibe with the idea that a powerful company has an obligation to behave in an open, fair way toward consumers and put their interests above its own.

While restaurant cleanliness can be managed with readily learned best practices (keep the raw chicken on a separate plate), doctors and lawyers face more complicated questions about what their duty to their patients and clients entails (should a patient with a contagious and dangerous disease be allowed to walk out of the office without treatment or follow-up?). But the quandaries of online platforms are even less easy to address. Indeed, one of the few touchstones of data privacy—the concept of "personally identifiable information," or PII—has become completely blurry, as identifying information can now be gleaned from previously innocuous sources, making nearly every piece of data drawn from someone sensitive.

Nevertheless, many online practices will always be black-and-white breaches of an information fiduciary's duty. If Waze told me that the "best route" somewhere just so happened to pass by a particular Burger King, and it gave that answer to get a commission if I ate there, then Waze would be putting its own interests ahead of mine. So would Mark Zuckerberg if hypothetically he tried to orchestrate Facebook feeds so that Election Day alerts went only to people who would reliably vote for his preferred candidate. It would be helpful to take such possibilities entirely off the table now, at the point when no one is earning money from them or prepared to go to bat for them. As for the practices that fall into a grayer area, the information fiduciary approach can be tailored to account for newness and uncertainty as the internet ecosystem continues to evolve.

Ideally, companies would become fiduciaries by choice, instead of by legal mandate. Balkin and I have proposed how this might come about—with, say, U.S. federal law offering relief from the existing requirements of individual states if companies opt in to fiduciary status.[2] That way, fiduciary duties wouldn't be imposed on companies that don't want them; they could take their chances, as they already do, with state-level regulation.

In addition, firms would need to structure themselves so that new practices that raise ethical issues are surfaced, discussed internally, and disclosed externally. This is not as easy as establishing a standard compliance framework, because in a compliance framework the assumption is that what's right and wrong is known, and managers need only to ensure that employees stay within the lines. Instead the idea should be to encourage employees working on new projects to flag when something could be "lawful but awful" and congratulate—rather than retaliate against—them for calling attention to it.

This is a principle of what in medical and some other fields is known as a "just culture," and it's supported by the management concept of "psychological safety," wherein a group is set up in a way that allows people to feel comfortable expressing reservations about what they're doing. Further, information fiduciary law as it develops could provide some immunity not just to individuals but to firms that in good faith alert the public or regulators to iffy practices. Instead of having investigations into problems by attorneys general or plaintiffs' lawyers, we should seek to create incentives for bringing problems to light and addressing them industrywide.

That suggests a third touchstone for an initial implementation of information fiduciary law: Any public body chartered with offering judgments on new issues should be able to make them prospectively rather than retroactively. For example, the IRS can give taxpayers a "private letter ruling" before they commit to one tax strategy or another. On truly novel issues, companies ought to be able to ask public authorities—whether the Federal Trade Commission or a new body chartered specifically to deal with information privacy—for guidance rather than having to make a call in unclear circumstances and then potentially face damages if it turns out to be the wrong one.

Any approach that prioritizes duty to customers over profit risks trimming margins. That's why we need to encourage a level playing field, where all major competitors have to show a baseline of respect. But the status quo is simply not acceptable. Though cleaning up their data practices will increase the expenses of the companies who abuse consumers' privacy, that's no reason to allow it to continue, any more than we should heed polluters who complain that their margins will suffer if they're forced to stop dumping contaminants in rivers.

The problems arising from a surveillance-heavy digital ecosystem are getting more difficult and more ingrained. It's time to try a comprehensive solution that's sensitive to complexities, geared toward addressing them as they unfold, and based on duty to the individual consumers whose data might otherwise be used against them.

TAKEAWAYS

In the absence of government regulations and widely accepted best practices for the use of personal information, companies should become information fiduciaries. This would mean acting in customers' best interest and putting their customers' interests above their own when conflicts arise.

✓ Ideally, companies will become fiduciaries by choice, not legal mandate.

✓ The fiduciary approach would give customers the right to know what data has been collected about them, the right to ask that it be corrected or purged, and the right to withhold certain data entirely.

✓ Instead of the hidden or obscure data harvesting that is now the norm, a fiduciary data gatherer would act more like a skilled hired professional, helping people whose data is in play to share what they are willing to share and no more.

✓ Information fiduciaries won't end targeted advertising, but they would prevent data from being used for purposes unrelated to the expectations of the person who shared it in the first place.

NOTES

1. Julia Angwin, Ariana Tobin, and Madeleine Varner, "Facebook (Still) Letting Housing Advertisers Exclude Users by Race," *ProPublica*, November 21, 2017, https://www.propublica.org/article/facebook-advertising-discrimination-housing-race-sex-national-origin.

2. Jack M. Balkin and Jonathan Zittrain, "A Grand Bargain to Make Tech Companies Trustworthy," *Atlantic*, October 3, 2016, https://www.theatlantic.com/technology/archive/2016/10/information-fiduciary/502346/.

Adapted from content posted on hbr.org, October 5, 2018 (product #BG1805).

TO REGAIN CONSUMERS' TRUST, MARKETERS NEED TRANSPARENT DATA PRACTICES

by Kevin Cochrane

I t's a good time to be a consumer. New digital business models have flipped the customer-brand relationship on its head. No longer do consumers need to do their own background research on a product or company to find what they are looking for. Instead, brands come to us. There are more options and more channels to get what you want than ever before.

That said, there is always a downside. This seemingly limitless digital economy has brought with it feelings of overexposure. No one likes to feel as if they're being watched, yet with technology continuing to mature, we have found ourselves entrenched in a marketing machine that has become far too intimate for anyone's liking.

The power of digital is so great that brands have started to abuse it. And with this abuse of power has come the erosion of the trust that once existed between businesses and consumers.

Over the last decade, businesses have built marketing technology stacks to collect and organize data with the hope of more effectively targeting consumers. Driven by the promise of loyal customers and greater revenue, it didn't take long for marketers to start using consumers' personal data without their knowledge or consent. What's more, the practice of buying data from third-party brokers become the norm, making customer and prospect data both stagnant and not earned. This ignited a dark process of monetizing consumers' digital lives that has quite simply backfired for companies.

As a result of using this inaccurate data, brands began to bombard consumers with messages that were not actually relevant to their personal interests. Rather than connecting authentically, brands became alienated from the individuals they were trying to reach.

The research bears this out: Nearly half of consumers say they have left a business's website and made a purchase elsewhere because the experience was poorly curated.[1] Further, 73% of consumers feel they haven't been engaged in a personalized way.

It's a tricky situation: Consumers want personalized offers that are relevant to their past behavior and future needs. To execute on this level of personalization, companies must collect large amounts of data. However, consumers want only *some* of their data used and only in a way that they are comfortable with.

So, what's the right way to navigate these complexities?

When done right, personalized messages can drive real revenue. Research from McKinsey found that personalization can deliver five to eight times the ROI on marketing spend and can lift sales by 10% or more.[2] It's clearly worth it for brands to invest in reconnecting with their customers.

To initiate a more trustworthy relationship, organizations must start by eliminating internal processes of acquiring third-party data. They must use only data that they have earned through explicit customer consent. Until now, the average consumer was likely unaware that when they "turn on cookies" it means they are agreeing to share their information with dozens—and in some cases hundreds—of affiliated partners. Those days are over.

Consumers should (and in the future will) have full visibility into how extensively their personal data is being monetized. This is an imperative, as research shows that 79% of consumers will leave a brand if their personal data is used without their knowledge.[3] With the European Union's General Data Protection Regulation (GDPR) officially implemented across businesses, brands have a fresh opportunity to reevaluate data practices, communicate them clearly to customers, stick to their word, and come out stronger on the other side.

GDPR and stricter privacy laws also mean that marketers will need to incentivize consumers to share their data. Consider the following best practices:

- Explain the benefits that customers will receive. Specific benefits might include more personalized offers, exclusive rewards, or access to a decision-making tool that makes life easier. Netflix is a great example: Without granting access to their personal data, customers would not benefit from Netflix's robust recommendation engine, which is a powerful way for consumers to discover new content that is highly relevant to their interests.

- Give customers full control over the types of data they share. Of course, certain types of data are more sensitive than others. Perhaps a customer is comfortable sharing their name and date of birth, but would rather not share their home address or mobile phone number. Putting the customer in control and providing flexibility in the types of data they are able to share makes it far more likely that they will offer up at least some personal information.

- Provide tools that easily allow customers to edit their privacy settings. To do this, organizations should consider implementing a digital privacy center where customers can easily understand and manage their data choices. Part of this should be the ability to configure exactly who within an organization has access to data. Additionally, it should include a "download my data" button that quickly and easily allows customers to know the exact information that a company has access to at any given time.

The final step is maintaining consistency. It's one thing for a customer to initially agree to data sharing but another for them to feel incentivized to continue to share it. Marketers can keep the relationship strong by adhering to privacy policies and providing consistent, valuable communication. Emerging technologies like artificial intelligence can help with this by building a single view of each customer that outlines all past behavior and communication with the brand. The way I see it, consumers will increasingly limit their brand loyalty to organizations that aid them with daily lifestyle goals. They will invest time and money in fewer but deeper relationships.

The digital era has fundamentally shifted assumptions for how individuals will do business and engage with companies. And once trust has been lost, it's nearly impossible for brands to rebuild sustainable, honest relationships with their customers.

As marketers, we must understand that real people buy from real people. This is why authenticity in marketing messages is so important, especially in the digital age. Transparency, consent, and trust are key to forming a long-lasting brand relationship.

As the industry becomes increasingly data driven, marketers must avoid becoming too scientific at guiding prescriptive outcomes. Rather, we should use data to relate at scale to individuals and to help guide them to self-discovered personal goals. Let's work to improve lives, not manipulate them.

TAKEAWAYS

Targeting customers has never been trickier. They want personalized offers that are relevant to their past behavior and future needs, but to do this, companies must collect large amounts of their data. Yet customers want only *some* of their data to be gathered and only in a way that they're comfortable with. How can marketers navigate these complexities and maintain a strong relationship with their customers?

✓ Companies should start by eliminating internal processes of acquiring third-party data and begin using only the data that they have earned through explicit customer consent.

✓ Customers should be given full visibility into how extensively their personal data is being monetized.

✓ Marketers should inspire customers to share their data by explaining the benefits that they will receive, giving customers full control over the types of data they share, and providing tools that easily allow customers to edit their privacy settings.

NOTES

1. Scott Tieman, "There's Power in Consumer Data. Is Your Brand in Control?," *Adweek*, May 13, 2018, http://www.adweek.com/digital /theres-power-in-consumer-data-is-your-brand-in-control/.

2. Matt Ariker, Alejandro Díaz, Jason Heller, and Jesko Perrey, "Personalizing at Scale," McKinsey, November 2015, https://www .mckinsey.com/business-functions/marketing-and-sales/our -insights/personalizing-at-scale.

3. "The 2017 SAP Hybris Consumer Insights Report: 1,000 Consumers Tell You What They Love and Hate About Brands," 2017, https://news.sap.com/wp-content/blogs.dir/1/files/SAP -Infographic-Consumer-Insight-Report-US_171220.pdf.

Adapted from content posted on hbr.org, June 13, 2018 (product #H04E2F).

8

HOW BLOCKCHAIN CAN HELP MARKETERS BUILD BETTER RELATIONSHIPS WITH THEIR CUSTOMERS

by Campbell R. Harvey, Christine Moorman, and Marc Toledo

Blockchain has important implications for marketing and advertising. But according to The CMO Survey, only 8% of firms rate the use of blockchain in marketing as moderately or very important.[1]

Blockchain technology is not well understood and is subject to a lot of hype. This combination creates a natural barrier to entry and has likely caused marketers to take a wait-and-see approach. However, there are many reasons to invest the time now to understand the technology and begin exploring specific marketing applications for your industry. Like digital platforms, social media, martech, fintech, and numerous other innovations, the spoils of blockchain may go to early adopters who commit to ruthless innovation.

Blockchain's properties—transparency, immutability, and security—make it reliable and trustworthy for applications such as supply chain management, smart contracts, financial reporting, the Internet of Things, the management of private (such as medical) information, and even electrical grid management. Meanwhile, its transmission model reduces the costs of transactions, enables verification and efficient exchange of ownership, and opens the door to real-time micropayments. Blockchain may make it possible for payment frictions to shrink, intermediaries to fade away, and consumers to own and control their personal information. In this, we see the disruptive potential of blockchain on marketing.

The Marketing Impact of Near-Zero Transaction Costs

Today, financial transactions have considerable costs. Retailers routinely pay credit card companies 3% payment-processing fees, while gas stations pay even more. Vendors using eBay and Shopify pay listing and sales fees, and consumers pay transaction fees on payment portals like PayPal. All these fees increase the cost of goods and are typically passed on to consumers. With the pervasive use of credit cards and debit cards, many merchants have set minimum purchases for their use to avoid having their profitability destroyed by fees.

Blockchain technology allows for near-zero transaction costs—even on microtransactions. Financial corporations like Mastercard and Visa already offer the ability to send money in any local currency over a blockchain rather than by swiping a credit card, taking advantage of the technology's additional layers of security and transparency. On top of that, being able to cut out intermediaries and directly connect the banks at both ends of each transaction can avoid most cross-border fees.

There are implications for marketers and advertisers as well. Marketers often try to get access to customer data by paying third parties (like Facebook) to share information. But blockchain could allow merchants to use micropayments to motivate consumers to share personal information—directly, without going through an intermediary. For example, a grocery store chain with a mobile app can pay users $1 for installing the app in their phones, plus an extra $1 if they allow it to enable location tracking. Every time they open the app and spend at least a minute on it, the retailer can pay them a few cents' or loyalty points' worth of store credit, up to a maximum per day. During that time, they push deals and special offers to the user. Indeed, user-tailored deals open a legitimate mechanism to deliver personalized prices that are a function of the consumer's profile. This approach has the potential to reduce the fraud and minimize the inaccurate or incomplete information from customers that currently plague these programs.

In the same way, marketers can enable *smart contracts* (virtual agreements that remove the need for validation, review, or authentication by intermediaries) that users can activate when they subscribe to email newsletters or sign up for a rewards program. Micropayments are deposited directly to the users' wallets whenever they interact with commercial emails—or with ads, which brings us to our next point.

Ending the Google-Facebook Advertising Duopoly

A similar model could be used with website ads by compensating consumers for each page view. In 2016, HubSpot published a research study showing that a majority of internet users dislike most forms of pop-ups and mobile ads and see online advertisement as intrusive and negatively disruptive.[2] An increasingly common response is to install ad blockers, a trend that is having a major punitive effect on the industry. It is estimated that ad-blocking adoption will cost publishers $35 billion by 2020.[3]

Blockchain-enabled technology potentially allows marketers to recapture some of that revenue with a different type of model: Marketers pay consumers directly for their attention and cut out the Google-Facebook layer.

We believe that the Google-Facebook duopoly in digital advertising will soon be threatened by blockchain technology. While keyword-based search will not disappear completely, it will become much less prominent. Eventually, individuals could control their own online profiles and social graphs.

With blockchain technology, companies can bypass today's social media powerhouses by directly interacting with consumers and can share the reward of ad exposure directly with them. In 2016, Google is reported to have generated an average of $73 per active user via ads.[4] Of course, the $73 is just an average over nearly one billion active users. It is reasonable to expect that Google brings in much more than $1,000 for certain highly valued demographics. Imagine the marketing possibilities when companies can efficiently transfer these values to consumers via willingly consumed advertising enabled by blockchain technology.

Blockchain technology can also verify ad delivery and consumer engagement; avoid ad or email overserving, which angers consumers and demotivates them from buying; and prevent follow-me ads that are no longer relevant (such as when consumers have already made a purchase of the company's or a competitor's products).

Ending Marketing Fraud and Spam

Fraud verification via blockchain will also help verify the origin and methodology of marketers. Micropayments will also effectively destroy the current concept of mass phishing spam, which dilutes the effectiveness of marketing for everyone.

Some 135 billion spam emails are sent every day, currently accounting for 48% of all emails sent. Spammers receive only one reply for every 12.5 million emails sent. A very small blockchain-enabled payment to the recipient of the email will discourage the spammer by increasing the cost of this activity. It should also help companies identify consumers who are interested in the transaction by their willingness to make this exchange.

Similarly, for the internet, every time a user clicks on a link, there could be a micropayment. In most cases, the user will make a small micropayment (for example, one cent to read a news article). This would defeat the denial-of-service attacks—a cyberattack in which bots hit a website with millions of requests, which causes the website to go down or to provide poor response time.

Blockchain could also make it difficult for bots to set up fake social media accounts, flood users with deceptive messages, and steal online advertising dollars from big brands. Online authenticity is baked into the blockchain technology. One company that is tackling the problem of social media fraud is Keybase.io, which enables individuals to use blockchain to demonstrate that they are the rightful owners of their various social media accounts. This will make the impact of marketing easier to track and marketing expenditures easier to justify—both are big wins for the profession.

As of 2016, $7.6 billion (or 56% of total display ad dollars) were lost to fraudulent or deceptive activity, a number that is expected to grow to $10.9 billion. By using blockchain technology to track their ads, marketing teams can retain control over all their automation practices, ensure that marketing spend is focused on ROI-generating activities, and directly measure the impact of marketing down to a per-user, per-mail metric. By tying user behavior and micropayments together, blockchain could solve the attribution problem that has bedeviled marketers for decades.

Remonetizing Media Consumption

Blockchain-enabled editorial content will likely allow companies to enhance quality control and copyright protection. For instance, (the reinvented) Kodak has created KODAKOne, which will feature a digital ledger documenting who owns the rights to individual images, allowing photographers to assert control over their work. Currently, the theft of online content is a pervasive problem and creators have little recourse to recoup lost monies other than expensive lawsuits. In the future, they will automatically and easily receive payments for content usage.

In addition, the average person who creates viral content, such as much-watched videos or social posts, could receive compensation for every click. (Currently, these creators receive little or no money unless their work is shown on online channels with subscribers.)

In all of these scenarios, content creators are empowered to produce relevant work that is valued proportionally to its success.

Companies like Coupit are getting ready to maximize the impact of that improved content. Its blockchain-based technology allows marketers to become part of loyalty and affiliate programs for opted-in consumers who can trade rewards with each other. Marketers gain visibility and transparency to differentiate between dormant and loyal customers, thereby expanding their strategies to send targeted offers to each group.

Even when a data aggregator or analytics intermediary is necessary, micropayments will allow companies to bypass ad blocking. Individuals will control the amount of personal information they share and will be directly rewarded for ad exposure, and many privacy concerns will be legitimately appeased.

One example of this is Brave, a new web browser created by Brendan Eich, cofounder of the Mozilla project and creator of the JavaScript language. Besides offering new levels of privacy and security, Brave is enabling a blockchain-based system aimed at transforming the relationship between users, advertisers, and content creators. Basic Attention Tokens (BATs) will allow publishers to monetize value-added services and capture some of the growth related to advertising, 73% of which is dominated by Facebook and Google.

Better Results for Companies and for Consumers

As blockchain goes mainstream, all intermediaries will need to adapt their business models. The decision chain will be structurally altered: Individuals will have more control over how they share personal information and how they spend their time interacting with advertisers. Spam and phishing scams will be stopped by their own nature—the more spammers spam, the more unsustainable they become from an economic standpoint. For companies, this could mean higher levels of control over the quality of inbound traffic for all their marketing efforts, as well as a much-needed improved understanding of customers' behavior.

On the other hand, exposure to advertisement will not be imposed without a transactional payment to each affected individual. Consumers will also have an incentive to post an accurate social profile online—detailing what they are interested in—because they will get paid for it. Marketers will be paying consumers directly—not the social media middle layer. When targeting high-value customers, the incentives will be accordingly higher.

Blockchain technology holds the potential for societies to become more trustworthy and empowered, increasing visibility, connecting parties, and rewarding individuals for their contributions to transactions. Marketing and advertising are fundamentally impacted by these changes. Finding ways to design and implement measures to make blockchain-related transformations should be a priority not only for CMOs but also for all strategic, financial, and technological decision makers. Operationally, companies may be able to build new levels of trust with individuals and ultimately connect their products and services with consumers in a manner and at a scale impossible to achieve without blockchain.

Marketing and technology leaders have the potential to leverage blockchain to reinvent their customer relationships. Early action on this far-reaching technology will put companies in the best position to benefit from what we think will be widespread adoption.

TAKEAWAYS

Blockchain could be a game changer for marketers and their customers because the transparency, immutability, and security it offers may make it possible for payment issues to shrink, intermediaries to become obsolete, and consumers to own and control their personal information.

- ✓ Blockchain technology allows near-zero transaction costs. Companies could use micropayments to motivate customers to share personal information directly, without going through a third party, or to pay consumers directly each time they view an internet ad, bypassing social media powerhouses.

- ✓ Companies can use blockchain to verify ad delivery and consumer engagement, avoiding ad or email overserving and preventing follow-me ads that aren't relevant.

- ✓ Blockchain can end marketing fraud and spam by collecting micropayments from spammers for every email opened and by making it more difficult for bots to set up fake social media accounts.

- ✓ Users can retain better control of their own intellectual property with the enhanced quality control and copyright protection blockchain-enabled editorial content offers.

NOTES

1. The CMO Survey, "Results," February 2018, https://cmosurvey
.org/results/february-2018/.

2. Mimi An, "Why People Block Ads (and What It Means for
Marketers and Advertisers)," *Hubspot*, July 13, 2016, https://blog
.hubspot.com/marketing/why-people-block-ads-and-what-it
-means-for-marketers-and-advertisers.

3. Jessica Davies, "Uh-Oh: Ad Blocking Forecast to Cost $35 Billion
by 2020," *Digiday*, June 7, 2016, https://digiday.com/uk/uh-oh-ad
-blocking-forecast-cost-35-billion-2020/.

4. "Google's Average Revenue per Monthly Active User from
1st Quarter 2015 to 4th Quarter 2016 (in U.S. Dollars)," Statista,
May 24, 2017, https://www.statista.com/statistics/306570/google
-annualized-advertising-arpu/.

Adapted from content posted on hbr.org, October 1, 2018 (product #H04K0R).

9

THE DANGERS OF DIGITAL PROTECTIONISM

by Ziyang Fan and Anil Gupta

Many governments are rethinking their policies regarding cross-border data flows. Although cross-border data flows grew by a factor of 45 between 2005 and 2014, according to a McKinsey analysis, events since 2014 have pushed the pendulum to swing away from unconstrained data globalization.

Some policy makers are concerned about individual privacy rights, consumer rights regarding the ownership of data, domestic law enforcement, and cybersecurity.

Others are driven by the desire to control or censor online media. Still others hope to create market barriers for global companies—a form of digital protectionism.

Our view is that too much regulation will create, in effect, data islands, trapping citizens and consumers on those islands and preventing them from enjoying the many benefits of tighter links to the global digital economy. These include access to digital goods and services, being part of global supply chains, accelerating and partaking in the fruits of innovation, and helping citizens access information, entertainment, and connectivity on a worldwide basis.

Data Is Deglobalizing

Many governments have started to question the merits of the unrestricted approach favored by the United States. Some, such as China and Russia, restrict the transfer of most types of data. For example, China's Cybersecurity Law, in effect since last year, requires

---

Authors' note: The views and opinions expressed in this article are those of the authors alone and not those of the World Economic Forum or the University of Maryland at College Park.

personal information and other important data to be stored within China.

While China's approach remains controversial even in China, other governments too are imposing various barriers to cross-border data flows. The most prominent of these is the European Union General Data Protection Regulation (GDPR), which took effect May 25, 2018. Aimed at strengthening EU residents' ability to protect their personal information, GDPR permits data transfers only to countries deemed as providing adequate data protection. Exceptions are permitted under certain conditions, such as in the context of binding and enforceable corporate rules.

In India, where the number of digital payments is growing by more than 30% annually, the central bank has ruled that digital payment enablers must ensure that all payment data is stored only on servers within India. Further, inspired by GPDR, a government task force submitted a draft of a broader personal data protection bill. While proposing that a copy of most types of personal data be kept on servers within India, the bill leaves it up to the government to decide which data cannot be transferred out of India at all. The draft bill has generated much debate, including some concern from global technology giants as well as Nasscom, India's IT industry body.

What Policy Makers Should Consider

Instead of either extreme—data islands or unfettered data globalization—policy makers should aim for more nuanced solutions. These solutions lie at the intersection of technology development by companies and policy formulation by governments.

First, policy makers need to adopt a risk-based approach. The flows of extremely sensitive data may need to be strictly controlled. Such data would include most types of personal information including gender, sexual orientation, health record, political orientation, and the like, in which specific bits of data are or can be connected to personal identifying information. For such data, the risks of cross-border sharing far exceed any likely benefits. At the other extreme, cross-border flows of certain types of private or public data, such as well production for a global oil producer or anonymous aggregated statistics, may be better left unfettered. For such data, the benefits of cross-border sharing far exceed any likely risks.

Second, a federated ecosystem model may be viable in those cases in which, though the data is highly sensitive, the benefits of data sharing are strong. The Beacon Project, spearheaded by the Global Alliance for Genomics and Health, illustrates how a federated model could work:

Data sets remain protected within national boundaries, but depending on the level of access granted to an organization, they can be queried individually or in aggregate through the Beacon Network. The World Economic Forum is spearheading Breaking Barriers for Health Data, a project that deploys federated database queries for transferring and processing health care data.

Third, in some contexts, a multinational company may be permitted to aggregate global data in a secure manner with the condition that a mirror image of the data pertaining to a country's residents be stored locally. India's finance ministry has proposed this approach to the central bank. The ministry's argument is that, unlike strict data localization, a mirroring approach would achieve both goals better—enabling the central bank to access payment data while also enabling Indians to benefit from integration with the global fintech sector.

Fourth, largely unfettered data flows should be part of regional trade agreements. The Comprehensive and Progressive Agreement for Trans-Pacific Partnership (the former Trans-Pacific Partnership minus the United States) includes explicit and binding language for cross-border data flows. The ongoing NAFTA negotiations also include provisions for the free flow of data. The European Union too is working on new provisions to be incorporated into all future trade pacts, aimed at striking a balance between the right to data protection and free digital trade.

Fifth, in contexts in which digital trade agreements do not exist and are unlikely in the foreseeable future, develop nonbinding norms and principles, leaving implementation to national governments. Global accounting standards have evolved through such a process. International Financial Reporting Standards (IFRS), a principle-based standard, are followed by over 100 countries. In contrast, the United States follows Generally Accepted Accounting Principles (GAAP), a rule-based standard. Slowly but steadily, the two sets of standards are converging. A similar bottom-up approach could play a role in the governance of cross-border data flows.

The Asia-Pacific Economic Cooperation (APEC) region, comprising 27 countries, including the United States, illustrates the potential for a bottom-up approach. APEC developed the Cross-Border Privacy Rules system, a principle-based framework for greater privacy protection as well as greater data flows.

Finally, as blockchain technology becomes more widely implemented, it could underpin some types of cross-border data flows. Blockchain ensures security, is tamper-proof, and enables the tracking of every transaction. Companies are rapidly adopting blockchain technology for the storage and sharing of global supply chain data. For example, some have started developing blockchain-based registries of every certified diamond in the world, enabling the complete tracing of a stone's movement from the mine to the consumer. Because blockchain relies on a distributed ledger system that is immutable and permanent, regulations to protect personal data will become essential when developing such solutions.

As every business becomes a data business, the future of globalization rests increasingly on cross-border flows of data rather than goods. Given the large and growing benefits of digital globalization, this is a welcome development. Yet valid concerns about risks to individual privacy and national security cannot be dismissed. Instead of an all-or-nothing approach, more nuanced solutions are likely to be the optimal ones.

TAKEAWAYS

Several governments have begun to question the unrestricted cross-border flow of data, but too many regulations could create data islands, trapping consumers on safe islands but cutting them off from the benefits of tighter links to the global digital economy such as access to digital goods and services. Policy makers should aim for more nuanced solutions to avoid the extremes of unfettered data or data islands.

- ✓ Policy makers should adopt a risk-based approach that controls the flow of extremely sensitive data, such as most types of personal information. For this data, the risks of cross-border sharing far exceed any likely benefits.

- ✓ For data that is highly sensitive but the benefits of sharing are strong, policy makers could create a federated model in which data sets remain protected within national boundaries but could be queried depending on the level of access granted to an organization.

- ✓ Policy makers should make largely unfettered data flows part of regional trade agreements. For contexts in which digital trade agreements don't exist and aren't likely in the foreseeable future, policy makers should develop nonbinding norms and principles and leave implementation to national governments.

✓ As blockchain becomes more widely implemented, policy makers should see where that technology replaces the need for cross-border data flow restrictions.

Adapted from content posted on hbr.org, August 30, 2018 (product #H04IRY).

WHY COMPANIES ARE FORMING CYBERSECURITY ALLIANCES

by Daniel Dobrygowski

I n the physical world, governments are responsible for keeping citizens and corporations safe from enemies. The digital world, so far, has been a little different. When it comes to cybersecurity and cyberattacks, most governments have spent much more time increasing their offensive capabilities than protecting companies and individuals.

The reason for this is that, until recently, national security officials viewed digital networks as fairly benign and cyberattackers as unlikely threats to safety—or to a country's sovereignty. However, the advent of cyber-physical systems and the Internet of Things, along with the increasing sophistication of bad actors, has made cyberattacks issues of human safety. But companies have largely been left to fend for themselves.

That's why, over the last few years, tech-focused companies have begun entering into cybersecurity alliances and pacts with one another. These alliances are a symptom of the breakdown of trust between policy makers and those they're making polices for. Hundreds of companies—some of them, such as Airbus, Cisco, HP, Microsoft, Siemens, and Telefonica, among the largest in the world—have tried to step into this trust gap by forming groups around goals related to the future of the internet and digital networks. Some of these groups (those I call the *operational alliances*) are mainly practical, sharing intelligence or technical data. Others (the *normative alliances*) are explicitly aimed at changing the ways companies deal with cybersecurity vulnerabilities and renegotiating the social contract between states and their citizens.

The operational alliances are built around small groups of companies. Their exchanges of information about cyberattacks and threats try to raise the collective level of cybersecurity, shape overall security practices, and speed the adoption of security technologies. Groups such as the Cyber Threat Alliance, the Global Cyber Alliance, and the Trusted Computing Group (to name a few) represent the range of such alliances.

For companies with IT or security departments capable of sorting through and acting on cybersecurity data, it often makes sense to become part of a network that can keep a CISO or IT team apprised of looming threats and best practices for mitigating them. The nature of digital networks is that everyone has to share the risks; these alliances help leaders share solutions, too.

The normative alliances, by contrast, make explicit calls for digital peace, government support for companies under attack, and cooperation to limit the use of private systems and networks against citizens (especially by a nation-state). They try to uphold values like trust and accountability in cybersecurity and to spur collective action in favor of peace and nonaggression—much as agreements between countries do.

Even so, these alliances vary in how much they presume to dictate corporate or even state behavior. The Charter of Trust, initiated by Siemens in 2018, favors self-regulation on the part of its corporate signatories that, over time, would establish expectations and norms that might apply to nations as well. The Cybersecurity Tech Accord, pioneered by Microsoft and other leading technology companies, aims to build "a safer online world by fostering collaboration among global technology companies"; its members pledge to oppose efforts by nations to attack citizens and enterprises.

These alliances are ultimately focused on the wider world rather than on individual companies and industries. The companies involved reason that working together gives them the ability to create the kind of safe, peaceful digital environment they need to innovate and protect their customers.

Yet while virtually every company supports peace, it may not make sense for every company to join one of these alliances. The charters and accords have the potential to put their signatories at odds with at least one national government, if not more. For those companies that operate the infrastructure of the internet, this dynamic already exists. The largest platform companies (like Google, Apple, Microsoft, and Facebook) increasingly find themselves in conflict with one or more major powers on policy or regulatory issues and the targets of sophisticated attacks. It is only by banding together and pushing for peace and security that they will be able to survive the seemingly lawless cyber environment. Companies that similarly will be targets of attacks (or that have customers who are) could see significant positive outcomes by joining these alliances, regardless of whether they confront their attackers.

Of course, not every company is so systemically important that it needs to take a position on the geopolitics of cybersecurity. Ultimately, it comes down to risk tolerance and capacity. It may be better for these companies to protect themselves as best they can through better cyber hygiene or by joining the operational and information-sharing alliances. These companies may prefer to sit on the sidelines for now, let other companies push the global conversation forward, and benefit from the increases in global security and trust that the alliances are starting to foster.

There is evidence that such efforts have indeed begun to move the conversation forward for companies and nations. For example, President Emmanuel Macron of France launched the Paris Call for Trust and Security in Cyberspace, a symbolic declaration to improve cybersecurity practices and international standards for the internet. Sixty-seven countries, including the entire European Union, have joined the pledge, along with 358 companies and 139 international and civil society organizations. (The list of signatories includes the World Economic Forum, where I am employed.) At the very least, the call represents an opening for companies and governments that care about security on a global scale to cooperate with a new set of allies.

That's not to say cooperation will be easy, or perfect, in the short term. Currently, the most powerful nations are signaling an aversion to cooperation on many fronts, not just in tech. Among the signatories to the Paris call, for example, three countries are noticeably absent: the United States, China, and Russia. Although the United States generally supports multistakeholder internet governance, China and Russia have opted for a more isolationist and state-controlled approach. Russia, in fact, has announced plans to develop the capacity to entirely shut itself off from the global internet, similar to the Great Firewall of China.

And even in spaces that are meant to foster cooperation among nations, there doesn't seem to be any patience for it. Given the past and continued shortcomings of state-only efforts to create cyber norms, one would think the benefits of working together are obvious. Instead, there are now two competing cybersecurity-norm efforts at the United Nations (UN): a Russia-sponsored Open-Ended Working Group, which includes China and is open to all interested UN members, and a U.S.-sponsored Group of Governmental Experts, which includes the European Union, Canada, Japan, and Australia.

Isolation is bound to be self-defeating since digital technologies derive most of their value from wider connectivity. In the worst case, digital isolationism fosters the logic of an arms race, in which state-directed hackers, hiding behind national firewalls, attack companies and governments seemingly with impunity. But no firewall is perfect, and such thinking will inevitably lead to conflict or a digital cold war. At the very least, isolation threatens to derail the benefits we've achieved through wider use of the global internet. Companies and individuals, the ones likely to bear the costs of conflict, should therefore continue to work together where they can. Cooperative efforts will keep up the pressure on governments to recognize that they are not the only actors who matter in the digital world.

Only cooperation can avoid a new age of global isolationism and digital conflict. The World Economic Forum's Centre for Cybersecurity is working to support new global architectures for security that recognize the reality of the digital world. In this reality, nations are just as important as they've ever been; they continue to be the ultimate protectors of their citizens. But civil society and companies are also important as the drivers of human rights and economic prosperity. What's needed now is cooperation on a larger scale, broader sets of allies working together to build trust and share responsibility, to protect the increasing numbers of citizens who rely on digital networks to survive and thrive.

TAKEAWAYS

The advent of cyber-physical systems and the Internet of Things, along with the increasing sophistication of bad actors, has made cyberattacks issues of human safety. Companies, left to fend for themselves by governments, have begun entering into cybersecurity alliances and pacts formed around goals related to the future of the internet and digital networks.

- ✓ *Operational* alliances are built around small groups of companies exchanging tactical and intelligence information, while *normative* alliances make explicit calls for digital peace, support, and cooperation.

- ✓ Alliances are focused on the wider world, rather than individual companies and industries, and work together to create the kind of safe, peaceful digital environment they need to innovate and protect their customers.

✓ Deciding whether to join comes down to your company's tolerance and capacity for risk—you may be able to protect yourself through better cyber hygiene or by joining operational and information-sharing alliances.

Adapted from content posted on hbr.org, September 11, 2019 (product #H055CF).

About the Contributors

ABHISHEK BORAH is assistant professor of marketing at the University of Washington's Michael G. Foster School of Business.

ANDREW BURT is chief privacy officer and legal engineer at Immuta.

KEVIN COCHRANE is chief marketing officer of SAP Customer Experience.

DANIEL DOBRYGOWSKI is head of governance and policy for the World Economic Forum Centre for Cybersecurity, where he advises on strategy, law, and policy around cybersecurity issues. His research areas include privacy, election security, intellectual property, competition law, digital trust, and governance of new and emerging technologies.

ZIYANG FAN is a lawyer and head of digital trade at the World Economic Forum. Formerly, he was senior legal counsel at Airbnb and assistant general counsel at the U.S. Trade and Development Agency.

ANIL GUPTA is the Michael Dingman Chair in Strategy, Globalization, and Entrepreneurship at the University of Maryland's Smith School of Business, cofounder of the China India Institute, and coauthor of *Getting China and India Right.*

CAMPBELL R. HARVEY is professor of finance and the J. Paul Sticht Professor of International Business at the Fuqua School of Business, Duke University. He served as the 2016 president of the American Finance Association. He is investment strategy adviser to Man Group PLC and partner and senior adviser to Research Affiliates LLC. Over the last five years, he has taught the blockchain course Innovation and Cryptoventures at Duke University.

LESLIE K. JOHN is a Marvin Bower Associate Professor of Business Administration at Harvard Business School.

KELLY D. MARTIN is an associate professor of marketing and Dean's Distinguished Research Fellow at Colorado State University.

CHRISTINE MOORMAN is the T. Austin Finch Senior Professor of Business Administration at the Fuqua School of

Business, Duke University, editor in chief of *Journal of Marketing*, and director of the CMO Survey.

TIMOTHY MOREY is vice president of strategy at frog, a global design and strategy firm. He leads a team of strategy practitioners who work alongside frog's designers and technologists to ensure the successful commercialization of products, services, and experiences. Tim speaks and publishes on strategy, innovation, and design. His research and article "Customer Data: Designing for Transparency and Trust" was a finalist for the 2015 HBR McKinsey Award.

ROBERT W. PALMATIER is professor of marketing, the John C. Narver Chair of Business Administration at the Foster School of Business, University of Washington. He is founder and research director of the Sales and Marketing Strategy Institute, a global organization focused on linking business and academics for knowledge. His research has appeared in a number of journals, and he has published books on topics including marketing strategy, relationship marketing, and customer engagement.

THOMAS C. REDMAN, "the Data Doc," is president of Data Quality Solutions. He helps companies and people, including startups, multinationals, executives, and leaders at all levels, chart their courses to data-driven futures. He places special emphasis on quality, analytics, and organizational capabilities.

MAURICE E. STUCKE is cofounder of Konkurrenz Group and a professor of law at the University of Tennessee.

MARC TOLEDO is a senior associate at PwC, where he focuses on blockchain and digital transformation. He is a Duke MBA graduate, and in his previous work at the World Bank and Apple he led large projects related to cybersecurity, machine learning, and artificial intelligence.

ROBERT M. WAITMAN is director of Privacy Insights and Innovation at Cisco Systems. He leads Cisco's Privacy Research Program and influences executives and other leaders on the economics of privacy.

JONATHAN ZITTRAIN is a professor at Harvard Law School, Harvard's John F. Kennedy School of Government, and Harvard's School of Engineering and Applied Sciences. He is faculty director of the Berkman Klein Center for Internet and Society.

Index

Is Your Business Ready for the Future?

If you enjoyed this book and want more on today's pressing business topics, turn to other books in the **Insights You Need** series from *Harvard Business Review*. Featuring HBR's latest thinking on topics critical to your company's success—from Blockchain and Cybersecurity to AI and Agile—each book will help you explore these trends and how they will impact you and your business in the future.

FOR MORE VISIT HBR.ORG/BOOKS

Engage with HBR content the way you want, on any device.

With HBR's new subscription plans, you can access world-renowned **case studies** from Harvard Business School and receive **four free eBooks**. Download and customize prebuilt **slide decks and graphics** from our **Visual Library**. With HBR's archive, top 50 best-selling articles, and five new articles every day, HBR is more than just a magazine.

Subscribe Today
hbr.org/success